INDIAN CINEMA BY PRIYANKA RAINA

INDIAN CINEMA BY PRIYANKA RAINA

PRIYANKA RAINA

ISBN 979-888546392-8

The Book "Indian Cinema by Priyanka Raina" is Dedicated to all Cinema Lovers who would love to read the means from where Cinema actually orginated, like the First Short film, First film, First Talkie film and prior to lots more.

Priyanka Raina

The Book is Dedicated to my Family for having faith in me and allowinf me to discover a world of glamour named "Cinema". Although first I learnt Theaters, studied acting before jumping into it.

- Priyanka Raina

Contents

Contents

Foreword

Priyanka Raina is a Indian film director and a Critic by her own terms as she loves reviewing movies based on content. Also in her reviews which are available on website www.themagicpr.com , she mentions "What's there in film" and "Weather you should watch or not?"

"Being myself a biggest Raj Kapoor fan in "Indian Cinema" so I always respect content based movies which leaves you with a certain messages. In recent years , there were more than 200 films releasing , from which at least 100 were worth watching.

Let me take privilege of introducing "Cinema" from where it all started and some of fantastic short films coming on board including the one made by me (Priyanka Raina) featuring Prem Chopra , Rakesh Bedii."- Priyanka Raina adds.

Lockdoown Short film 2020

Preface

"Indian Cinema – By Priyanka Raina is a book written by Author Priyanka Raina where Book tells on how Cinema actually started to Era of "Black and White" films taking to "Color" era.

Director's Cut

Priyanka Raina is a Indian film director and a Critic by her own terms as she loves reviewing movies based on content. Also in her reviews which are available on website www.themagicpr.com , she mentions "What's there in film" and "Weather you should watch or not?"

Acknowledgements

Trilok Chand Raina

The Book "Indian Cinema – By Priyanka Raina" is all about journey of Girl who shares her vulnerable experiences on her love Indian Cinema. I dedicate my book to my Papa Trilok Chand Raina who's my inspiration that made base in Mumbai, and privileged to being brought up in Mumbai. And then "Where there's a will, There's a way" and with your passion and dedication you can always achieve your goals.

Starting from a scratch to entering into biggest Bollywood parties can be a dream for anyone, right?

This book will share global experiences , talks with veteran Directors Subhash Ghai sir, Actor Jeetendera Sir who were like Biggest support in supporting my Short films

(Priyanka Raina)

Prologue

The Book "Indian Cinema By Priyanka" is all about How Cinema was started in India way back in 1896 with the very first short film to first film to first Talkie film , taking from Black and white to Color Era and when the First Superstar was formed.

The book is about lots more about telling journey of Priyanka Raina who was Born into Defense family in Mid 80s , so its almost impossible to Discover myself and watch the "Old Classics" of Cinema . But Time went well to come across different phases of life which eventually made me fell in Love with my wonderful "Cinema".

Cinema is the biggest means of Entertainment and we in Bollywood are proud to share more than 100 years of Entertainment. This Book "Indian Cinema" is about Journey of Girl "Priyanka Raina" to her journey of Directing Short Films, Assisting in Feature Films, Interviewing the Legendary filmmakers, Talking on Cinema on Rarest films. In short, you name the film and she has the answer.

Priyanka Raina in her 90s Childhood with Parents

CHAPTER ONE

Start of cinema

Taking you right back to the Eighteenth century Era when one day a guy was watching a "Pea plant" growing. Daily he use to see a d take pictures imaging its growing. Then in year 1896, when "Pea Plant" grew up , He gathered all the pictures one after one in form of a "Slide" and then played. He was actually happy to see his "Documentary" in form of a film.

He was called "Lumiere Brothers", and hence he named his Documentary as "Birth of a pea Plant" which eventually became the very First Documentary in History of Indian Cinema

Lumeire Brothers

And hence the history was created, The beginning in "Indian Cinema" by this camera where pictures were framed One by One in form of "Slide" and then use to see through the "Hole" on a big screen made of "White paper".

This was the first camera

But all this "Drama" was noticed one person who was at time Assisting the due. He then went to London to know more about filmmaking where he was offered to "Direct" films for them on his excellence knowledge.

But at the moment he thought , if I have so much knowledge then why I should make "Cinema" for your country. I will make movies from my country so he took Camera, Editing machines and came to India . He is known as "Dadasaheb Phalke", his incredible journey of giving Birth to "Indian Cinema", first film, first talkie film and lots more apart– We will see in next chapter .

Priyanka Raina at Dadasaeb Phalke Awards 2011

CHAPTER TWO

Birth of Indian Cinema [Black &white to Color]

As we saw in previous chapter, Dadasaheb Phalke packed his bags with few instruments like Camera, Editing techniques and came to India in Nashik – A place in "Maharashtra". Nashik is also the Birth place of Dadasaheb Phalke, so he decided to open a studio at his Home itself.

Henceforth he constructed a small studio, where use to do rehearsals for a certain play which he was planning to transform into movie. Here as at that time, there were restrictions for Female artists, so there were "Males" playing characters of "Females". And he created a Twenty minutes story title "Raja Harishchandra" which was a silent film. Actors acted just with Expressions. "Raja Harishchandra" was released in Theaters on 3rd Mar 1913 with giving Birth to Indian Cinema , and very first film of Indian Cinema Directed by Dadasaheb Phalke.

Raja Harishchandra

Although after this, journey for Dadasaheb Phalke never stopped. He Directed many plays, movies where Males were playing roles of Females.

Here he brought his wife "Saraswatibai Phalke" in frame who eventually became first Women Editor as was supporting Dadasaheb right from Mixing to Film-Developing chemicals, perforating raw film sheets at night by Light of a candle. Holding White Bedsheets for hours in Blazing Sun as Light reflectors, and she also cooked for film unit for about 60-70 people.

This time Dadasaheb thought, its high to give its First female actor to Indian Cinema, Because every time males cant play their roles – As it was more funny. Then in year 1913, he introduced movie "Mohini Bahamasur" which became the first Women oriented film in Indian Cinema.

First Women film "Mohini Bahamasur"

Mohini Bahamasur is 1913 Indian Mythological film, Directed by Dadasaheb Govind Phalke starring Kamlabai Gokhle and Durgabai Kamat, who eventually became the first Women Artist in Indian Cinema. As Mohini Bahamsur is first Indian film to have a Female actor. As In Raja Harishchandra, role of female actor was played by Anna Salunke, a male actor.

Now ,Dadasaheb though that It was the time to give sound to Indian Film Industry so he started researching on Sound and Created Bombay Talkies Studio. Under Bombay Talkies, First Talkie Film ALAM ARA – Directed by Ardeshar Irani was released in 1931. The Film ALAM ARA starred Prithviraj Kapoor, Zubeida

Although Prithviraj Kapoor acted previously too in silent films like College Boy and Sher a Arab as tweeted by Rishi Kapoor in reply to Priyanka on social platforms.

Rishi Kapoor ✔ @chint... · 05 Nov 19 ⌄
No Priyanka,"Alam Ara"was the first talkie film of India in which he worked as a character actor. Earlier to that, he had bit roles in about 8-9 films in which "College Girl"and "Sher-e-Arab"were notables before he hit stardom in "Vidyapati".I stand to be corrected if wrong.

Priyanka Trilok Raina · 05 Nov 19
Replying to @RishiKapoorFC1 @PrithviTheatre and 6 others

Yess.... ALAM ARA featuring Prithviraj kapoor and Zubeida (Rhea Dutt s grand mom)
Directed by Ardesher Irani

♡ 19   ⟲ 27   ♥ 431   ⟨⟩

Enter Caption

Then after this Era almost started with the most beautiful moves , Music that touched souls Starring Actors unlike Dilip Kumar , Raj Kapoor, Ashok Kumar, Nargis Dutt, Nutun and many more till we came to Color Era.

Kisan Kanya was a 1937 Color film which was directed by Moti Gidwani and produced by Ardeshir Irani of Imperial Pictures. It is largely remembered by the Indian public on account of it being India's first indigenously made colour film

V Shantaram had earlier produced a Marathi film *Sairandhri* (1933) which had scenes in color.[1] However, the film was processed and printed Germany *Kisan Kanya* was, therefore, India's first indigenously made color film. Kisan Kanya was based on a novel by Saadat Hasan Manto and focussed on the plight.

Researched on History of Indian Cinema

Just when my review of DHOBIGHAAT was published in renown magazine, they loved my writing. So told me to write on "History of Indian Cinema" as Industry was completing 100 years. On this I was pretty confused and told, "But I don't know anything about cinema. Am totally blank".

On this Editor told, "Priyanka you have Internet. Everything is there online. First research and then give a good write up. This also will be knowledge about Cinema". I finally agreed and started reading about cinema first and believe – It was a fruitful. Wrote a article in Two days time and it was published.

Priyanka Raina At Dadasaheb Phalke

The Indian film industry is the largest in the world (1200 movies were released in the year 2002)[citation needed]. India also features the cheapest cost of tickets in the world (the average ticket cost only 20 US cents), and the biggest movie studio in the world, Ramoji Film City [citation needed]. The industry is supported mainly by the vast cinemagoing Indian public, although Indian films have been gaining increasing popularity in the rest of the world — especially in countries with large numbers of expatriate Indians.

Regional film industries

A cinema hall in Delhi India is a large country where many languages are spoken. Each of the larger languages supports its own film industry: Urdu/ Hindi, Bengali, Marathi, Kannada, Tamil, Telugu, Malayalam

Art cinema

In addition to commercial cinema, there is also Indian cinema that aspires to seriousness or art. This is known to film critics as "New Indian Cinema" or sometimes "the Indian New Wave" (see the Encyclopedia of Indian Cinema), but most people in India simply call such films "art films".

From the 1960s through the 1980s, the art film was usually government-subsidised: aspiring directors could get federal or state government grants to produce non-commercial films on Indian themes. Many of these directors were graduates

of the government-supported Film and Television Institute of India. Their films were showcased at government film festivals and on the government-run TV station, Doordarshan. These films also had limited runs in art house theatres in India and overseas. Since the 1980s, Indian art cinema has to a great extent lost its government patronage. Today, it must be made as independent films on a shoestring budget by aspiring auteurs, much as in today's Western film industry.

The art directors of this period owed more to foreign influences, such as Italian Neo-Realism or the French New Wave, than they did to the genre conventions of commercial Indian cinema. The best known New Cinema directors were Bengali: Satyajit Ray, Ritwik Ghatak, and Bimal Roy. Some well-known films of this movement include the Apu Trilogy by Ray (Bengali), Meghe Dhaka Tara by Ghatak (Bengali) and Do Bigha Zameen by Roy (Hindi).

Art cinema was also well-supported in the state of Kerala. Malayalam movie makers like Adoor Gopalakrishnan, G. Aravindan, T. V. Chandran, Shaji N Karun, and M. T. Vasudevan Nair were fairly successful. Starting the 1970s, Kannada film-makers from Karnataka state produced a string of serious, low-budget films. Girish Kasaravalli is one of the few directors from that period who continues to make non-commercial films.

Birth of Indian Cinema

In the year 1896, Dadasaheb Phalke just noticed Pea plant growing , and made the First ever Documentary "Birth of a Pea Plant". Then Dadasaheb went to London to gain further knowledge and to screen "Birth of a Pea Plant".On seeing , he was invited by Hollywood to Direct for them. Dadasaheb clearly mentioned that I will make only Indian films, for my country and returned with camera . So made a Silent Film Raja Harishchandra , which gave Birth to Indian Cinema Released on 3rd May 1913. In this film , male actors only played Females .

Then Dadaji thought , now its time to give Female Actor to Industry and so made Mohini Bahamasur and Introduced forst ever Actress to Indian Film Industry,

Now , It was the time to give sound to Indian Film Industry so he started researching on Sound and Created Bombay Talkies Studio. Under Bombay Talkies, First Talkie Film ALAM ARA – Directed by Ardeshar Irani was released in 1931. The Film ALAM ARA starred Prithviraj Kapoor, Zubeida. Here counting one more not which recently Rishi Kapoor sir tweeted in reply to my Tweet. Rishi Kapoor said , "No Priyanka , Alam ARA was the first talkie film of India in which he worked as a character actor. Earlier to that, He had bit roles in about 8-9 films in which College Girl and SHer –e-Arab were notables before he hit stardom in Vidyapati. I stand to be corrected if wrong.

Priyanka with Rishi Kapoor and Neetu Kapoor

And Then Journey of Indian Film Industry began with Dilip Kumar films , Raj kapoor which was golden Era of 1950-60s. Seen movies featuring Raj Kapoor – Nargis Dutt, They looked so stunning in Awara, Barsaat, Andaaz, Chori Chori, AAH, Shree 420 and many more.

CHAPTER THREE

Music in Indian Cinema

Raj Kapoor Incredible friendship with Majrooh Sultanpuri gave us precious Treasures in Indian Cinema !

"The cinema that was made by **"Raj Kapoor"** will always be special in History of Indian Cinema , and guess when we will see those cinematic days in todays cinema ",

Being a Raj Kapoor fan , sharing a trivia about how it all started . As we all know that Raj Kapoor movies had incredible music, songs which melted our heart. And it all started when a struggling lyrics writer **Majrooh Sultanpuri** came into the eye as he was trusted friend of **Jaddanbai**.

Nargis Dutt 's Mom JADDANBAI

Jaddanbai was Nargis Dutt "s Mom who use to accompany her to sets .As Raj Kapoor and Nargis Dutt were shooting two movies at that time, One day when Jaddanbai could not go to sets , so she requested her assistant writer MAJROOH SULTANPURI to go to shoot. The film then being made was AAG, which was produced and directed by Raj Kapoor.

Starting with poetic conversation on sets, soon Raj Kapoor asked him to pen a song on situation and Majrooh Sultanpuri wrote song "Raat ko ji chamke taare". This song was recorded by composer Ram Ganguly in the voices of Mukesh and Shamshad Begum.

Now Raj Kapoor loved the way Majrooh used to pen songs and soon he became the solo lyricist of ANDAZ which was produced and directed by

Mehboob Khan, which was released in same year of Raj Kapoor's Barsaat where he introduced another fresh pair of lyricist HASRAT JAIPURI and SHAILENDRA.

Picture is from "Raj Kapoor Memorial" in Pune SET OF AWARA with Priyanka

However Raj Kapoor was observing Majroh Sultanpuri 's rapid progress as when he wrote poem against Jawaharlal Nehru at meeting orgaised for mill workers in mumbai where he clearly mentioned him as "Hitlor".

Majrooh was asked to apologize , and he refused to do so saying "Writer has no limitations" and he was jailed. In jail, when Raj Kapoor went to visit him and he asked, "So Mr. writer , what is the song that you have been thinking about current situation?

On this Majrooh incidentely wrote "DUNIYA BANANEWALE KYA TERE MANN MEIN SAMAYI , KAAHE KO DUNIYA BANAAYI" which was then penned for Teeseri Kasam movie. The song meant "O creator of this world, what came into your mind? Why did you create this world." .

Raj Kapoor imediately paid him 1000 rupees for that song which was quite high that time as lyrics were paid only 150 Rupees. With the permission of Majrooh Sultanpuri , Raj Kapoor appointed Lyrics writers Hasrat Jaipuri and Shankar Jaikishan for finishing of song. This song was then sung by Mukesh and composed by Shankar Jaikishen.

In 1973, Raj Kapoor signed Majrooh Sultanpuri for his own production RK BANNER with the movie Dharam Karam which was directed by his son Randhir Kapoor.

RK BANNER

Majrooh then wrote the iconic legendary song EK DIN BIK JAAYEGA sung by Mukesh which became a huge classical song for years. So this was how Raj Kapoor immense love for Music in Indian cinema , and we got some incredible songs to be loved forever. And Majrooh Sultanpuri hence wrote all songs for RK Banner .

Raj Kapoor Statue of EK DIN BIK JAYEYEGA

Isn't that an Incredible Love for cinema which would be remembered for years, guess when we will get those days back where Love had no boundaries.

We are all aware of our first ever Showman **Raj Kapoor** who did not just make movies , But although he created an Era – A Masterpiece with a unique message. From where to start, Right from 50s magic with Barsaat , Andaaz , AAH, Shree 420, Awara, Chori Chori to Mid Age 60s -which started with Dharm Karam, Jis Desh mein... finally flew with Biggest ever Hits of 70s with Bobby , Ram teri Ganga Maili, Mera naam Joker , Prem Rog and many more. If you get STATUES and SETS of all above , wouldn't it be amazing feel ?

"BOBBY" immortal

So Here we go , RAJ KAPOOR MEMORIAL situated in MIT University campus in Pune. From being a Fan Girl to my journey as Director , had an opportunity to Visit Raj Kapoor Memorial . As I entered , first saw lovely immortal of Raj Kapoor and Krishnaraj Kapoor – which gave a smile on my face

Then followed by is the lovely journey of all Raj Kapoor films , made in the form of statues- Decorated with piece of art and lights and Music revolving around. In Music , can hear Historic journey for Raj Kapoor.

Stars were Born

First superstar

In

Indian

Cinema

Rajesh Khanna

Now in previous chapter , we have seen about "Showman" Raj Kapoor who introduced new means of Cinema with films enriched in Content and Music. Music that can wave your hearts.

That was time when they were less actors and people were Bored of seeing new faces, so a Association named "Bombay Films Association "introduced a Contest through advertisements in 'Times of India'. This brought in new charms from different states in India.

First Superstar who was loved overnight by people, where women use to keep his photos under their pillow was 'Rajesh Khanna'

Rajesh Khanna

Rajesh Khanna was the First Superstar who acted in about 159 films, Co produced films and produced as well. He was married to Dimple Kapadia and has two daughters Twinkle Khanna (Who herself is Author now) and Rinkie Khanna.

Well , Rajesh Khanna met Dimple Kapadia in thoroughly a filmy style. This happened when Dimple Kapadia was travelling in flight for her Bobby promotions and Rajesh Khanna requested her "Can I sit here" and Dimple's joy knew no bounds. Like when any other girl's dream was to sit with Rajesh Khanna and then how can Dimple refuse. So here's the love story began.

Well Rajesh Khanna's first film is Aakhri Khat in 1966 which got him to through Bombay Association contest

Aakhri Khat

Prior to that , Rajesh Khanna acted in couple of films unlike Raaz, Aurat , Baharon ke Sapne, Shrimaan ji , Bandhan but his Claim to fame became

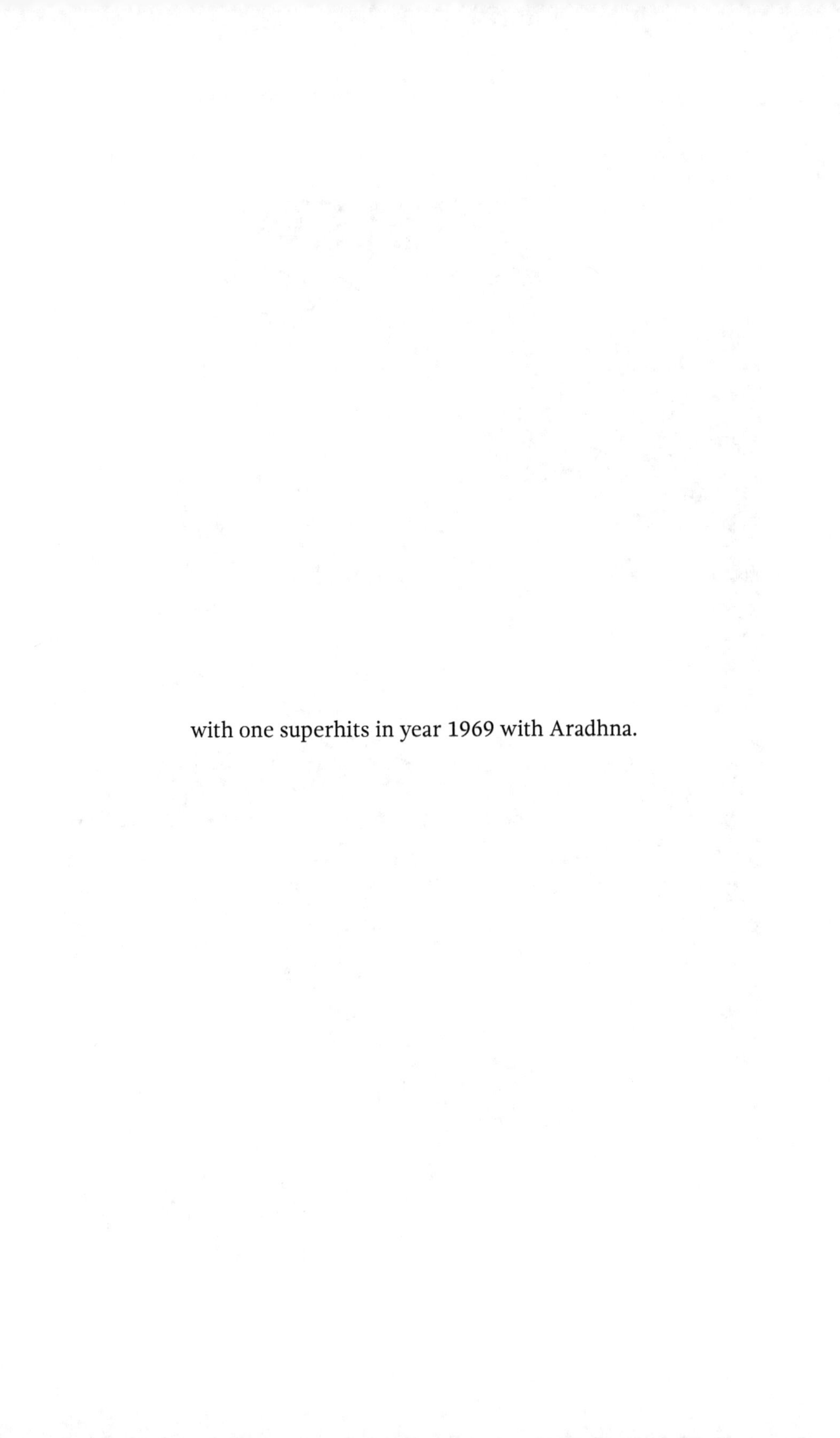
with one superhits in year 1969 with Aradhna.

Shakti films
aRadhana
Produced & Directed By : Shakti Samanta
Music : S.D.Burman
Lyrics : Anand Bakshi
DVD

Aradhana

Hence in year 1969 itself , Five movies Ittefaz , Do Raaste , Doli Bandhan in row released for **Rajesh Khanna making him the First Superstar in Indian Cinema**. in next year 1970 itself , Rajesh Khanna had six amazing films like Train, Sacha Jhootha, Aan milo Sajana, Kati Patang, Safar Khamoshi which were all 'Superhits'. With this Rajesh Khanna was also also as 'Hit' machine who would deliver 'Hits' in a row.

Year 1971 saw Ten Rajesh Khanna films with Hits like Haathi mere Saathi , Andaz, Choti Bahu , Maryada, Dushman carrying on with most prestigious film 'Amar Prem' in year 1972. Also Amar Prem has this iconic song 'Kuch to Log kahenge' which meant a lot. Henceforth journey continued when Legendary Yash Chopra signed Rajesh Khanna for his First movie DAAG in 1973.

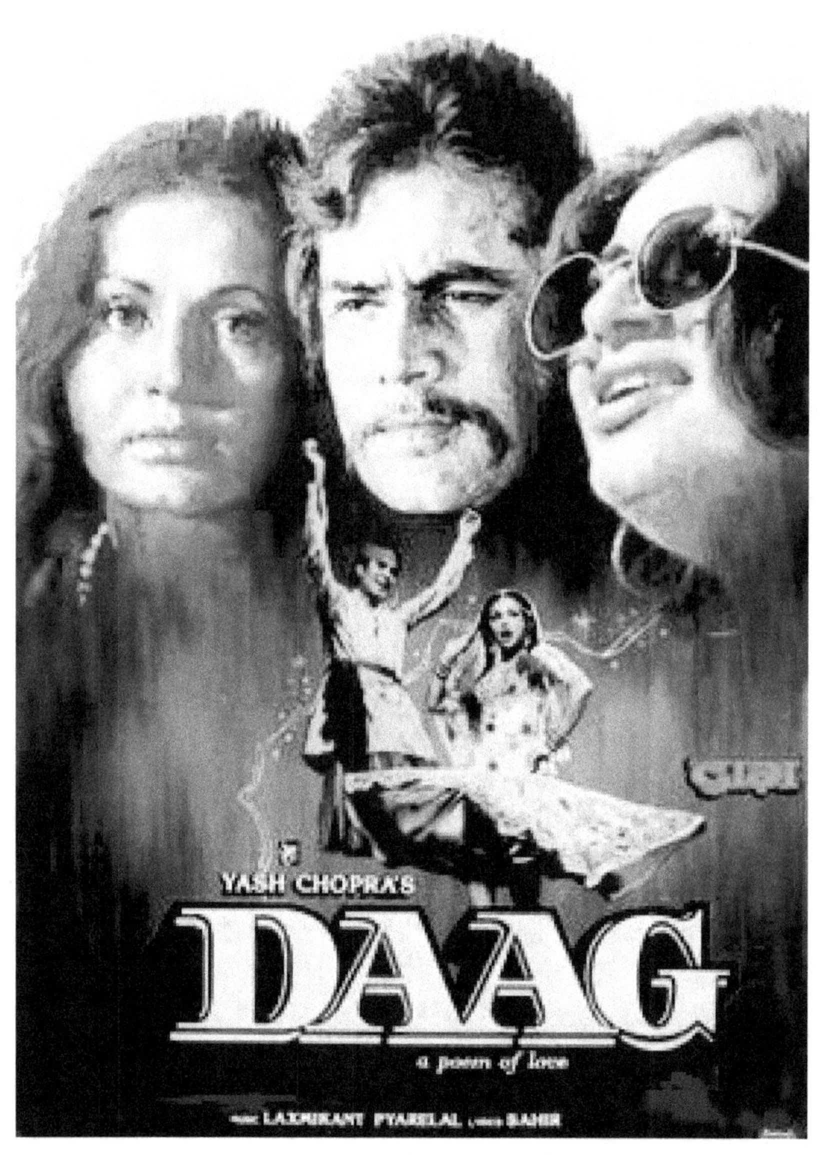

DAAG

Also DAAG feature film was first film of No 1 Production House YRF. Here Rajesh Khanna also becomes Superstar to do a very film for production which later became No 1 production.

Also in year **1973** itself, Rajesh Khanna got married to Dimple Kapadia. This happened when Dimple's first film "Bobby" was releasing featuring **'Rishi Kapoor'** who yet has another history.

Rajesh Khanna, Dimple Kapadia

Then coming to years from then after 1974 , Superstar Rajesh Khanna had some amazing films unlike ROTI which also he coproduced as well. Prem kahani, Aavishkar added more flavours and that's the reason its known as Era of 'Mega70s' . Also in this era, college boys used to have Hair cut of Rajesh Khanna style.

1980's changed Rajesh Khanna's style of portraying Elder characters in "Avtar" "Souten" and many more considering the most stylish and message oriented film with "Swarg" which was also introduction of Govinda, Juhi Chawla as fresh pair.

Swarg

Rajesh acted alongside Mumtaz in eight films. They were neighbours and got along very well, which translated onto the screen. Mumtaz stated "I would pull his leg and tease him about his fan following. Whenever Rajesh entered a hotel in Madras, there was a queue of 600 girls waiting to see him at midnight. As a result, even I would get some importance, as people would ask for my autograph as well. He was very generous with his associates, and would party a lot.

During the peak of his career he would be mobbed during public appearances. Fans kissed his car, which would be covered with lipstick marks, and lined the road, cheering and chanting his name. Female fans sent him letters written in their blood.[57] There used to be a line of cars of his producers and hysterical fans outside his bungalow every day. Actor Mehmood parodied him Bombay to Goa where the driver and conductor of the bus were called 'Rajesh' and 'Khanna' respectively. Even today, he remains the favourite of mimicry artists, who copy his trademark style and dialogue delivery.

During the filming of *Amar Prem* there was a scene that needed to be shot at Howrah bridge with a boat carrying Khanna and Sharmila under the bridge. The authorities ruled this scene out as they realised that if the public found out that the star would be there, it may create problems on the bridge and that it might collapse due to the number of people trying to get a glimpse of their favourite actor.Film critic Monojit Lahiri remembers "Girls married themselves to photographs of Rajesh Khanna, cutting their fingers and applying the blood as sindoor. Rajesh was God, there has never been such hysteria."

In the year 1974, the Filmfare Awards were held honouring the films released in the year 1973. Khanna was nominated for his performance in a complicated role in *Daag*. However, since Rishi Kapoor had paid Rs.30,000 to receive the Best Actor award for his role in *Bobby*, Khanna did not win the award for his performance in *Daag*

Several songs sung by Kishore Kumar in the 1970s were based on Rajesh Khanna. During the filming of the song "Mere Sapnon Ki Rani" in Aradhana, Sharmila Tagore was shooting for a Satyajit Ray film and director Shakti Samanta had to shoot their scenes separately and then join the scenes together. In the 1970s, his chemistry with Sharmila Tagore, Mumtaz, Asha Pareikh, Zeenat Aman, Tanuja and Hema Malini were also popular with audiences.

In 1973, BBC also made a documentary on him named as *Bombay Superstar* as a part of their *MAN ALIVE* series. Shooting began when he got married and his film *Daag* premiered. In the video it can be noticed that Khanna was shooting for *Aap ki kasam*. A textbook prescribed by the Mumbai university contained an essay, "The Charisma of Rajesh Khanna!"

Sharmila Tagore said in an interview to *THE INDIAN EXPRESS* that "women came out in droves to see *Kaka*. They would stand in queues outside the studios to catch a glimpse, they would marry his photographs, they would pull at his clothes. Delhi girls were crazier for him than Mumbai girls. He needed police protection when he was in public. I have never seen anything like this before or since.

Music remained one of the biggest attractions of all Rajesh Khanna films throughout his career. His films were always known for the music with chartbuster soundtracks. The reason for this was that Khanna used to personally sit in music sessions with music directors such as Kalyanji Anand ji,

R D Burman, Shanker Jaikishan, Lamikaant Pyarelal, S D Burman, Bappi Lahiri and select tunes for duets and solo songs in his films. He used to be personally present for recording of the solo songs to be picturised on him.

Later in the year 1990's Rajesh Khanna also joined 'Congress' for five years , due to which he lost his bit stardom

Rajesh Khanna

Then he left politics and carried back to acting playing a substantial role in movie AA AB LAUT CHALEN which is Directed by Rishi Kapoor and is featuring Akshaye Khanna and Aishwarya Rai.

Then Rajesh Khanna continues with acting only and never said 'Yes' to politics and his Daughter Twinkle Khanna was launched in Barsaat, along side Bobby Deol. Twinkle Khanna is married to Akshay Kumar who is well known actor today.

His younger Daughter Rinkie Khanna who appeared in fewer films and later she too got married to a Businessman in London.

Dharmendra

Prior to **Rajesh Khanna** Another Hero who was introduced through 'Bombay films Association' is Punjabi LION mostly known as "He-man of Indian Cinema", Our Beloved Dharmendra Deol. Here we have an incredible story.

Once Dharmendra orginal born as "Dharam Singh Deol" told his Mom that he will go to Mumbai to become hero. His Mom told, "Ok but first you atleast give some letter that you are coming" . On this Dharam Singh Deol replied, "It's not like that. You will have to go and struggle".

Few days later his Mother words guessed were heard by "Bombay film Associaton" as they announced a contest "Actors wanted" and here we got a another star as "Dharmendra"

Dharmendra

Dharmendra started off from small roles with "Jitne dood jitne paas" in 1960. For few years he struggled off with small roles until he played as "Lead" actor in "Begaana" as Prakash in 1963.

Begana

And then the journey never stopped , Dharmendra acted in several Hit films unlike Dharamveer , Aaye din bahar ke, Deval , and many more.

Now while Dharmendra was sitting on narration of "Sholey", he saw that movie has two characters "Jai" and "Veeru". So he told Ramesh sippy, that I know one guy, He is tall and good looking. If you like him, you can get Jai and here's how **Amitabh Bachchan** was introduced as Angry young Man.

Dharmendra , Amitabh Bachchan

Dharmendra's first marriage was to Parkash Kaur at the age of 19 in 1954. He had two sons from this marriage, Sunny Deol and Bobby Deol Deol both successful film actors, and two daughters, Vijeeta and Ajeeta. His nephew Abhay Deol is also an actor.

Dharmendra then launched Sunny Deol in Betaab, Directed by Rahul Rawail and produced by his Production "Vijeyta Films".

Betaab featuring Sunny Deol and Amrita Singh

Also Dharmendra acted in many films with Sunny Deol incuding the one "Saltanat" where also Shashi Kapoor's Son was introduced along with beauty queen "Juhi Chawla"

Saltanat

After moving to Bombay and getting into the film business, **Dharmendra** was always in news as married Hema Malini with staying married to his first wife without having to get a divorce although. Also then Dharmendra launched his second son Bobby Deol along side Rajesh Khanna's daughter Twinkle Khanna in Barsaat under his production "Vijeyta films"

Dharmendra and Hema Malini starred together in a number of movies in the early 1970s, including *Sholey and there love was immortal.*

Dharmendra , Hema Malini

The couple has two daughters, Esha Deol (an actress, born in 1981) who was launched with "Koi mere dil se pooche" and "Na tum jaano na hum" in 2001 and Ahana Deol (an assistant director, born in 1985).

Dharmendra's grandson and son of Bobby Deol, is also named "Dharam Singh Deol" after Dharmendra. In 2019, Dharmendra's grandson and Sunny Deol's son Karan Deol made a debut withPal pal dil ke paas[1]

JEETENDRA

Another "Star" in 70's and 80's prior to Dharmendra and Rajesh Khanna is most commonly known as 'Jumping Jack' , None other then Jeetendra. With whom I share an incredible bond as my First Serial was Balaji Telefilms - The Production which was launched by Jeetendra with longest running show on ZEE 'Hum Paanch' . It was then carried forward by his Daughter Ekta Kapoor, who took it to waves

BEING
PRIYANKA

Jeetendra , Priyanka Raina

Also Jeetendra has set another trend of White pants which was famous amoung the college goings in those days

Now Tushar Kapoor too launched his own production with the very first film 'Laxmi"

Rakesh Roshan

Another association whom not much , but met a fewer times is Rakesh Roshan Sir at pre launch events.

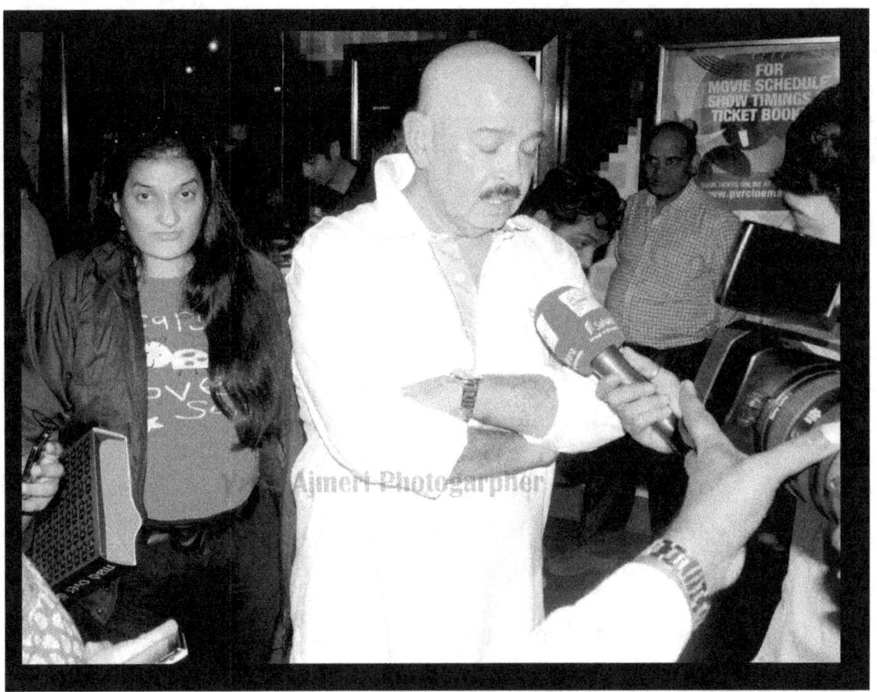

Rakesh Roshan

Rakesh Roshan started off as an actor , But in no time Switched to Direction making some of biggest hits like Khudgarz, ,Khoon Bhari Maang, Karan Arjun.

Here Rakesh Roshan's story is also slight like Raj Kapoor. Like After 'Mera naam Joker' flopped and He was having no funds. So Raj Kapoor decided to make story with new comers, So Bobby Happened.

Similarly after Koyla flopped, Rakesh Roshan had no money to sign Stars, so decided to write a first love story with New Bees. Here Rakesh Roshan never ever thought of Hrithik as he never wanted him to enter into Acting. But tables said something else.

Hrithik had done a acting course while he was studying and when came to know that his Dad is looking for new comers, so he quitely showed his certifcate to his mom, Pinky Roshan. She was suprised and told Rakesh that once take test of Hrithik. When Rakesh Roshan saw Hrithik, he was suprised and told "Beta when did you do course"

But he was happy , and write entire story according to Hrithik Roshan and here's how star was born

Hrithik Roshan , Priyanka Raina

Hrithik Roshan Bagged four Best Actors awards in Decade , becoming the
Superstar of Millenium ans also the most handsome man in world

CHAPTER FIVE

Childhood Means of Cinema- Priyanka

Born into Defense family in Mid 80s , so its almost impossible to Discover myself and watch the "Old Classics" of Cinema . But Time went well to come across different phases of life which eventually made me fell in Love with my wonderful "Cinema".

Baby Priyanka Raina

Firstly, let me justify that it's our INDIAN CINEMA and not "Bollywood'. During this lockdown 2020, I was actually discovering about myself on seeing my past journeys, my short films, my feature films, advertisement that am actually being part of – and just thought to share my views to you. Especially to those who doesn't belong to Mumbai and still can be part of our 'Cinema' through digital world.

Cinema is the biggest means of Entertainment and we in Bollywood are proud to share more than 100 years of Entertainment. This Book "Indian Cinema" is about Journey of Girl "Priyanka Raina" to her journey of Directing Short Films, Assisting in Feature Films, Interviewing the

Legendary filmmakers, Talking on Cinema on Rarest films. In short, you name the film and she has the answer.

First attraction as Child were Epic "Ramayana" and "Mahabharata" in early 90s where I have seen roads emptying out on Sundays when Episodes use to run on Doordarshan on Black and White Television. Henceforth seeing transformation from "Black And White' to 'Color Television' through various means of Entertainment like Chitrahar, Surabhi to SHANTI , Swabhimaan , Chandrakanta to Hum Paanch which were longest running television shows of Mid 90s.

Now Coming to First feature film which had seen is none other then "Hum Hain Raahi Pyaar ke' in 1993. The movie came into my minds because the Girl out of three Kids was from my school and Two years elder then me. Hence would hear from friends in school (Auxiluim Convent) about the movie, Talking about it and so on. That days as was no Internet that I could "Google' so came Home and switched on Television to see Movie advertisements. After a Bit, The song came and guess my First Attraction with Juhi Chawla. Simply fell in love with the song and The Actor of coarse Aamir Khan Sir whom I always admire for Content.

Juhi Chawla , Priyanka Raina

Of coarse HUM HAIN RAAHI PYAR KE did not see at theaters, But the First seen movie as a child was "Hum Apke Hain Kaun" with full family. And also HUM APKE HAIN KAUN became the first and only film to be seen with full family, because some of films hardly you can see with family. And

Last year was blessed to see HUM APKE HAIN KAUN again in theaters as celeberated 25 years wit entire cast.

Celeberating 25 years of HUM APKE HAIN KAUN

So Here got finally Name of "Juhi Chawla" in Indian Cinema as child and started seeing her major movies. As mostly of her films were with Sunny Deol and Rishi Kapoor , And from Here 'Heroes' came in picture when saw TU TU TU TARA on screen. Also then first ever movie to see in Theaters with Family was "Hum Apke Hain Kaun" , But that time too small to understand the meaning of emotions.

I had issue , if I like any particular actor's movie. I scroll back to see what movies done in Past. Accordingly when scrolled back QSTK , Saltanat came into league. Then almost seeing all movies of Sunny Deol and Rishi Kapoor after seeing "Damini" ; "Bol Radha Bol" , "DARR" including Debuts Bobby, Betaab and many more in 90s were getting on Discovery Mode to my Globalized Cinema. And song from "Najayaz" gave first glimpse to Ajay Devgn. Growing up with these actors seeing some amazing Content made my Goals more strong to Enter in Bollywood. That time I didn't even dream of Bollywood. I always said, "Want to become Computer Engineer when I grow up" .

During my 10th standard saw first glimpse of movie "Kaho na pyar hai" and ran to brought the cassette . Fell in complete love with Blue eyes of Hrithik Roshan. Use to dance on beats of Kaho Na Pyar hai . My First attraction towards Hrithik Roshan.

Priyanka Raina , Hrithik Roshan and Sahila Chaddha

Kaho Na Pyar Hai released on 14th Jan 2000. This was only movie which I saw in May after SSC Board got over. Movie saw in Plaza Theater booked by Family.

As entered into the world of SIES College in 11th, By that time had made my minds for acting but told at least will complete 12th. When joined degree college that time curiosity increased to Enter the world of Dreams just happened

One day while at NIIT was sitting with my friends gossiping , Sir came and said "Priyanka , you got a good height and can just walk the ramp for us as we have shortage of a girl". And while walking ramp , I discovered myself while everyone was cheering "This is so cool , I want to be part of this"

Priyanka Raina

CHAPTER SIX

To Be part of this Beautiful World called "Bollywood' wasn't so easy for an outsider, But not impossible at all because 'Where there's a Will, there's a Way". Also this question would be too in minds of millions users , Searching for a platform , 'A Source' where they can set their dreams.

So My Goals were set, and During College days say in 2004 started researching on Internet "Which is nearest Acting Classes" and was thrilled when Answer came 'Chembur'. Scrolled more and found "Ashok Kumar Acting Institute". Before going saw few Ashok Kumar films just to know more about him so am not Total Blank. Saw 'So Din Saas ke', Aradhna, dream Girl , Tawaif and many more to get idea. Guess was totally impressed by Acting and Entered into his bungalow (That Time was Bungalow , Now Converted into Towers) .

When Enquired to Join Class , was told to go back stage which was behind the Bungalow; There a Lady was sitting named Preety Ganguly (Daughter of Ashok Kumar) . She replied politely , "One Batch is starting from Tom if you wish you can come from tomorrow" . My Excitement knew no bounds as was entering the First stone towards my dream.

In Acting Class , learned several words which are used in Shooting like Scripting , Diction (Speech) , Improvisation (Where a scene is given to you and in act according to your situation) , Meditation (Very important as its gives Concentration while rehearsing Dialogues, Getting into the scene). Also very important one, learned to frame a song according to situation. I was given song "Jadu sa chaane laga..." so had to act in this song.

Priyanka clicked during Acting workshops

Well , Prior Acting class as was in college that time so quietly auditioned at Balaji Telefilms.

My joy knew no bounds when Got a call from the most Popular and prestigious show "Kyunki Saas bhi Kabhi Bahu thi" which eventually became my college fame. Prior Then 'Proxies' came for college and was in Balaji Shoots doing small characters.

Still from Kyunki sas bhi kabhi bahu thi

Scene from KYUNKI SAAS BHI KABHI BAHU THI , with Gauri Pradhan

When College got over , Thought these small roles can't take me to achieve my dreams so left everything and joined THEATER World. Learning with Ekjute at Prithvi Theaters was almost a fantastic tuning with mazing friends Sushant Singh Rajput, Richa Chaddha and all.

At theaters learnt to be disciplined, How to get patience while performing your dialougues, Creating a scene.

Enter Caption

While at Prithvi (That time wasn't knowing that this place belongs to Kapoors but use to love the ambience) got a pass for SAWARIA premiere party.

I said to my self , "Which industry I am entering, first let me see from close" and then was all into the Biggest ever Premiere Night.

Walking into the Red Carpets with crowd gathered (Wasn't knowing that time that it was Media) and since I was having pass so no one stopped me. Walked straight on Red Carpets where on Gate Sanjay Leela Bansali along with Ranbir and Sonam were standing to welcome guests.

They saw my pass and said "Welcome" . Inside was a star studded party and was knowing no one, so nervous went and stood quietly next to Rani Mukherji. Next to Rani was Sonam , Ranbir and at few cm away Priyanka Chopra. Waiters were serving food in Tray, but was feeling awkward to eat so said 'No Thanks'.

Then Sanjay Leela Bansali was making announcement "We are starting movies in screen 2 and screen 4, so please get in to your screens" . He came to me and asked, "Beta which is your screen" (Saw my Pass) "Ohh Screen 3" and said "Oh You have time, Enjoy the party".

Something magical while entering the screen 3. Since all elder actors were there in Screen 3 so Salman Khan was standing on gate and welcoming and sending them in. We all were standing in line , Ahead of me was Dimple Kapadia and Salman sent her in. Then Salman saw me and smiled and I smartly told, 'I am to theater actor , you can carry same procedure with me too'. Then Salman Khan gave hug and said "Please come". And that's how was my first interaction with Salman Khan.

Have lots of memories which are still alive in minds about SAWARIA premiere, which was my very first Premiere party while learning Theaters. In interval as was standing on First Floor of (Imax) looking down , guess what Saira Banu came and stood besides me. She asked ,"Beta you seem to be new"

I Replied , "Nothing just am a Theater student. So just watching my industry which I will be part of very soon"

Saira Banu liked my confidence , she continued to chat with me talking on my adventures , About me , Etc. Remember at a distance of 10 cms dilip Kumar was walking and looking at Both of us when we were busy in chats.

When movie was over , remember we all were coming out silent with a blank expression. Then one actor came and told me , "Please don't go, Ranbir is coming personally to everyone to know the feedback". Was pretty nervous that what would I say , seriously my face was showing it all. Could see Ranbir going to every one – Karan Johar, Assistants , Directors to know the feedback.

Then Ranbir Kapoor came to me and Still remember his words as first party is always special. Ranbir holded me and said, "So tell , How did you like the movie"

In a pretty nervous mode looking at his eyes, I said "Loved the Dance especially DEKHO CHAAN AAYA and you entry in JAB SE TERE NAINA was crowd pulling. You were fantastic and have a long way to go"

Ranbir was guessing something about movie, but I did only said about him. He smiled and said "Thanks for a genuine feedback" and gave a hug. Some moments are always special and this was my moment. As a theater student , to get opportunity of World's Biggest Premiere Party "Sawaria"

Ranbir Kapoor , Priyanka Raina at BR STUDIOS

This pic was clicked later while Dubbing at BR Studios. But that was my first ever chat with Ranbir Kapoor. Could see his dedication, enthusiasm towards his goal, His Love towards 'Cinema' Just like me.

CHAPTER SEVEN

How direction comes into pipeline for an actor and association with media starts

An audience is always attracted towards the glamour and talk about the smaller cities, Every single watches film for Rishi Kapoor or Dhamendra or may be any actor. No one remembers the name of a Director. And when decide to enter Bollywood on what want to become? The answer is only one- Hero.

I was in same situation when decided to come into acting, was pretty confused. My Theaters got completed and got a small character with 10 day movie outdoor shoot. I was just excited about the word "Outdoor". Movie was just a picnic where every morning spot used to knock door to say "Breakfast". After breakfast we use to make a round of shooting that when is our role , followed by Chatting. Thankfully Movie actually never released. I came back and said , "This is not I want to do, This will never make me Hit my dreams".

So left everything and quietly joined Graphics course where learnt 3DS MAX, Sources of Editing in Premiere Pro, FLASH, sketches and all. Although when completed course , made my First short film in Animation titled "Azaad Bharat" (12 mins) . Azaad Bharat is a story of Pre Independence Era to till India got its independence. All this moments showed through Animation. Azaad Bharat released on 15th August 2010.

My first animation poster - AZAAD BHARAT

TO make a Animate film took 6 months and that's how where actually I had put on weight. Then decided to make regular films and enough of Animation as didn't want to put weight on.

Friends recommended to come to Dubbing studios where post production of film 'Honour Killings' was going on. Working on Honour Killings , I had collaborations with actors Prem Chopra, Gulshan Grover who were part of movie too. The movie is directed by Avtar Bhogal , silently use to listen how he is handling Dubbing, coordinating with Actors.

Priyanka Raina with Director AVTAR BHOGAL

Honour Killings Directed by Avtar Bhogal was to screened at IFFI GOA and they invited me to be part of promotions. Indeed was my first ever visit to Goa and was pretty excited to meet people around. When Was walking down Red carpet with a glamorous outfit, had so many clicks – They must be thinking that I am Actor of a Festival film.

Priyanka Raina at IFFI GOA

My life has been blessed with special moments to be cherished upon. Also once I was in GOA for Location visit for a small short shoot. Got a call from Ajay Devgn 's Office , "Priyanka , Congratulations you have won the contest and we would be Happy to see you tomorrow at SUN N SAND"

On this I replied , "But I am in Goa". Immediately said "Don't worry , Goa is not too far. I will see you tomorrow" .

Now this is also a story. Ajay Devgn Sir has put a contest on Facebook for ONCE UPON A TIME IN MUMBAI to write anything on Life of 70s because that's what the movie was based on. And when comes to Writing I wrote a nice paragraph.

Cut to Next Day : As I entered JUBLEE ROOM in Sun N Sand , Saw Ajay Devgn sir sitting right on Sofa. His manager told, "Priyanka came" . On this Ajay sir told, "Let her relax, have tea or coffee. We will start in five minutes".

That time wasn't comfortable of having anything outside so told "Just water" and sat quietly. So the moment came when shared the most iconic frame with King of Bollywood. Also on moment I told Ajay Devgn, "Sir am totally new with no experience. Have written a story for feature. If u can just read and guide me weather its good or not"

Meet with AJAY DEVGN

On this Ajay Devgn immediately told to contact manager. And can you guess next day itself got a call "Priyanka , please give your story that you told Ajay Devgn". My excitement knew no bounds and went with a draft of 99 pages. That movie was never made as not satisfied with the ending but my 'Introduction' of Ajay Devgn's character was used in DIL TO BACHCHA HAI JI.

Well that was a sweet journey which started bounding with friends along, Until my First feature film as assistant Director 'Daal mein kuch kaala hai' started which released on 29th july 2012.

Press conference of first film as AD "Daal mein kuch kaala hai"

Also here I learnt proper screenplay writing, framing , Narration to actors is an important aspect to filmmaking. But Like other assistant didn't wanted to tie myself into just assisting. So made a small Short film "CLEAN AND GREEN INDIA" which is another story coming up in another chapter, How idea of short films came to my mind

Clean and Green India (Short film)

Also by the time, Bonding with media was rolling up. One day while I was sitting at Prithvi Theater, Got a call from Number 1 Magazine "Priyanka , can you go to see a movie"

I got surprised and said "Movie....?"

Editor replied , "It's the screening and movie name is Dhobighaat"

I told instinct, "But Who will allow me...?

On this Editor gave the name of person and tell him may name, no one will stop you. And I reached PVR JUHU where the screening was. Although the publicist told screening hall was full, But I was least bothered as met my Ajay Devgn office mates so busy chatting.

Further Publicist told, "Don't worry , will arrange a another screening for you guys"

And we left down stairs. But within ten mins got a call on my mobile, "Priyanka we have arranged screening for you guys and starting movie within Half Hour. Reach YRF studios"

Its was my very first screening so it has to be special from somewhere in the skies, isn't it?. And I entered YRF studios to watch DHOBIGHAAT – My first Press show.

Priyanka's First Screening of DHOBIGHAT at YRF

CHAPTER EIGHT

Making of "Clean and Green India" too has another story. Since had made song through animation in AZAAD BHARAT, so this time was planning to record an Album. Considering the Budget was going too high , But was surrounded with good friends in the industry to guide.

They Questioned:

Q : Why you want to make an Album?

A : Want to shoot next...

Q : Are you lyrics Writer?

A : No

Q : Are you a Music Director?

A : No.... I am Director

Then told, You are Director , A writer so write a small story and take this camera , Shoot and show us weather you can control unit or not. That's how mission began.

Then How Idea of 'Clean and Green India' derived?

That time "Anna Hazare" moment was going on, which I was very much part of ralleys. So did a bit ANDOLAN towards Swatch Bharat. Also we went to RALLEY GAON pune, where thrilled to see cleanliness. Understood one Motto "Cleanliness Begins at home"

Priyanka at RALLEY GOAN, Pune

Anyone use to smoke or through Garbage on road, would tell "Please though in Bins". Then thought for a moment "I am a filmmaker not a politician, so will tell through my wonderful means of Cinema"

Hence story of Clean and Green India was written which is a Three minute short film

Making of CLEAN AND GREEN INDIA

After shooting was complete, For Editing my studios was Booked at BR Studios, where again met Ranbir Kapoor. Guess he was dubbing for WAKE UP SID that time

At BR studios

Then process of 'Filmmaking' Dubbing , Background Score , Mixing and all. Making Short films helps to learn every aspect of filmmaking rather than attending a Theory class.

Since Clean and Green India was on message and my first , so wanted to censor. Directors gave agent number , But I wanted to see White house. They understood Excitement level . Sharing address old, "Good , you can go . That's how you will learn" . Then my Three minute short film was on Censor office for two weeks. I was tensed that why not calling me.

Then on 28th Sept 2011, got a call from Censor Board, "Priyanka , your short film 'Clean and Green India' has been censored . please come and collect your film". Couldn't tell my excitement level, as it was a baby start to filmmaking . Getting censored was just like a dream and when was clicking pic there, One filmmaker said "First time, I know. Could feel the joy on face"

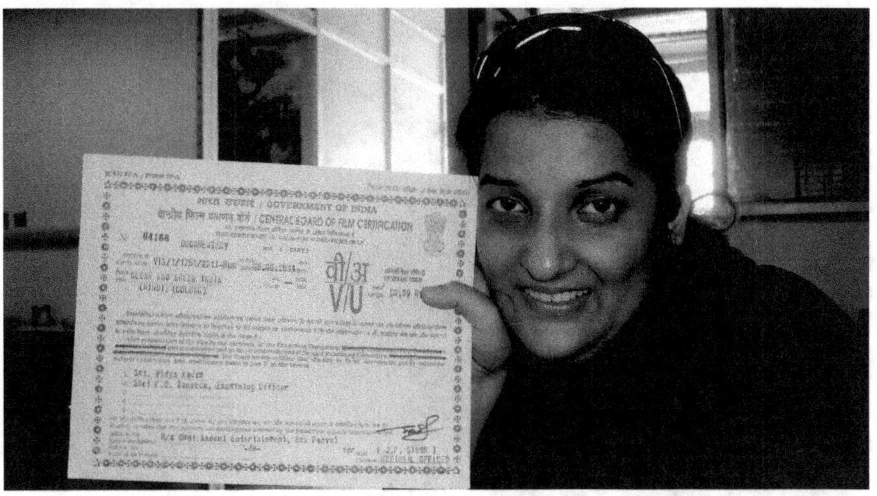

My first censored short film CLEAN AND GREEN INDIA

Later realized 28th Sept was same date in 1973 when iconic BOBBY released and its also Ranbir Kapoor's Birthday. And Clean and Green India became my First censored Short film.

Editing of CLEAN AND GREEN INDIA at BR studios

Also with it , Blessings of Legend were important. One day , YRF team invited me to YRF studios on 4th Floor. Yes it was same place where Yash Chopra 's cabin is there. When was having my 'Black Coffee' , Yash Chopra talking on phone came and stood besides me.

At YRF studios

I got up. On this Yash ji told, "Beta, Coffee we should sit and take".
I replied , "Sir in front of you how can I sit"
Then Yash Chopra sir smiled and patted (Giving Blessings) . Although
it was short meet of 15 mins , But was fruitful to be with Legend.

Priyanka with legendary Yash Chopra

Then was never stopping moment. Wrote then short film DUM which was on life of "What students do after finishing college" , Struggles and how they finally overcome it. DUM was first ever short film to shot in Iconic Prithvi Theater else they hardly allow camera there. If you want to see Old Prithvi Café, Library, Its premises and watch my DUM and feel the ambience. Dum was released by Vetern Actor Manoj Kumar sir on his Birthday 24th July 2012

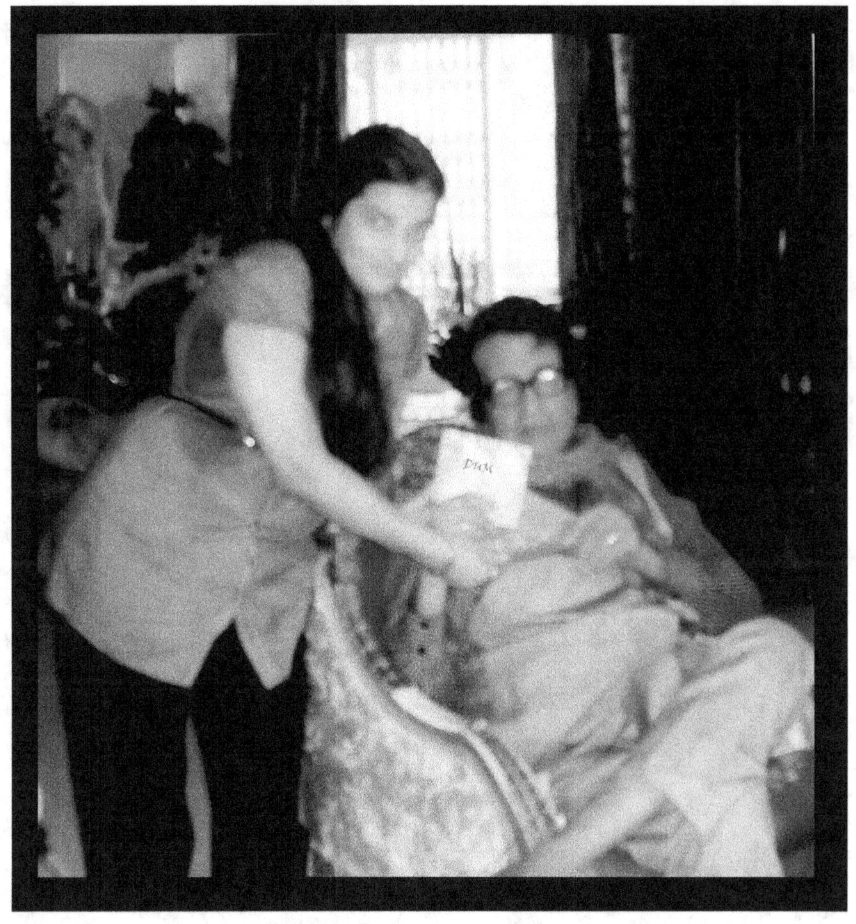

With Legendary Manoj Kumar

Until then was already into "Black Currency" team to be directed by Sanjay Sharma. By the time I already started reviewing films in Media and Interviews with Bollywood actors which will be sharing in another section.

Coming to filmmaking , Here friendship began with his younger Brother Kapil Sharma on talking filmmaking notes. I just shared an idea that in one home whole family of ten members are staying. What problems they must be facing? One Bread earner to feed many and was done. Our Producer Kirdar Ali who came to Sanjay Sharma's office only liked the idea and decided to produce.

Then Kapil Sharma wrote the screenplay for film and we began meetings to finalize cast of film, Technical crew like Cameraman, Lights department, Makeup and vice versa. That's how my Biggest short film ZINDAGI happened in league.

"Shooting of Zindagi was the best phase of life , as I was directing a short film on larger scale with all Renown actors. Discipline was maintained but at time was fun too"-Priyanka Raina

Enter Caption

Also Zindagi gave me appreciations in lots of Films festivals , became headlines in Media and became a short film to Hit a huge of 45 Milion hits on social media.

Zindagi (12 minute) Short film became the biggest grosser hitting 46 million on you tube which gave huge articles in Top publications.

Zindagi written by Kapil Sharma and Directed by Priyanka Raina . Featuring Hum apke Hain Kaun actress Sahila Chaddha, Yuvraaj Parashar, Preety in lead roles. This short film created waves in media . Will be sharing some of interviews of veteran Directors as we wind up

Manoj Kumar viewing screening of my Zindagi.

Priyanka with KC Sharma , Sahila Chaddha, Sanjay Sharma and Kapil Sharma

Manoj Kumar , I saw his movies only when they made fun on 'om Shanti om' just to see who's the actor so saw Purab aur Paschim , Kranti, Roti kapda aur makaan, Shaheed , and guess totally turned out my Idol Diretor as loved his style of taking.

Manoj Kumar with ZINDAGI

Subhash Ghai sir called me at his residence in Bandra ,and as I walked in – Actor Kartik Aryan was sitting (That time Kaanchi released) . I was sitting with kartik Aryan , when Subhash Ghai sir was telling about kanchi.

I clearly remember his words, 'Kaanchi will my last film which I had directed , now will be heading only training students and producing films because if I continuously making such films , People will forget my Epic films that I had made ."

What a truly words by Legend , Truly admire Subhash Ghai Sir

Subhash Ghai with ZINDAGI

Priyanka Raina, Subhash Ghai

CHAPTER NINE

First Mami with Yash Chopra

After attending IFFI 2010, was fascinated towards film festivals as lots of meet up happen. Attended Mumbai Film Festival in 2011, but that time was well planned. MAMI 2011 happened at Chandan (Juhu) and PVR (juhu) will well constructed meets.

Dia Mirza , Priyanka Raina

In between us, was vacant for Yash Chopra sir who was yet to come. MAMI 2011 had lots of memories like seeing French Film "THE

ARTISTS" with Yash Chopra sir .

Priyanka Raina With French film Director Micheal

Also after festival when was in Lift with Yash Chopra sir along with Amit Khanna sir, I told "Sir till date just heard about you that you choice is Brilliant. Today I saw if Yash sir likes a film, it has to be brilliant"

On this Yash Chopra smiled and said , "Thanks" . By the time lift doors were open and we moved out.

Lighting Lamp at MAMI

Glad to share these small moments as Blessings of MAMI 2011 and would tell to youngsters that set your target first and ways open accordingly

Highlights of MAMI 2011 with Shabana Azmi

CHAPTER TEN

AD SHOOTS

First AD film did was with California based Director Upinder Raisddun as Advertisement for astrology. Did Two AD films with him as Assistant Director. AD world is although a different experience as you have to shoot according to seconds. Firstly Assisted in ASTROLOGY AD film .

Astrology AD with California based Director Upinder Raisuddin

Apna Bazaar Advertisement ,I had acted too where played the role of Photographer (Girl in blue Shirt). It was although a different experience when Upinder Sir told, "Priyanka , In Apna Bazaar giving you role too. But don't wear anything green as it's a Chroma shoot."

Apna Bazaar AD

Studying graphics and then shooting in CHROMA is technically with lots of Homework. You have to be clear with your shots shooting in front of Green cloth because later Image in background will come (Which is your locations)

Also Assisted in one Advertisement Directed by Prabakar Shukla and Gautam Bhatia. This was another Dream come true as had opportunity to work with (MAINE PYAR KIYA) girl Bhagyashree

Priyanka Raina, Bhagyashree

Also worked on one Documentary "Swantra senani" which shoot was held at MAD ISLAND. Here too was different experience working on scripting, narrations, seeing online editing and accounting. Ravindra Arora who was production controller here and Documentary was under Ramesh Meer sir.

Swantra Senani , Directed by Ramesh Meer

CHAPTER ELEVEN

Interviews Meet and interview with Dharmesh Darshan

The Seasoned Director Dharmesh Darshan Speaks up exclusively on his Journey ," I believe GOD CREATES

The Seasoned Director, **Dharmesh Darshan** who has given all Good Actors to Indian Cinema in form of talent – Creating a HISTORIC films like **RAJA HINDUSTANI, DHADKAN** and many more ; Speaks up to **Priyanka Raina**

Enter Caption

Priyanka Raina: Dharmesh Ji , Tell us something about our unique journey till now. You are the only film maker to have directed few films & almost all are hits.

Dharmesh Darshan: Yes, I am the only Writer/ Director who has done six films Beginning with early 1990s. I would like to tell you about – Starting with LOTEERE Starring Sunny Deol, Juhi Chawala, Nasseredin Shah & Then Cam to Raja Hindustani

Priyanka Raina: (Cuts) Raja Hindustani ..... The Mega Blockbuster, The only Film which created History Worldwide.

Dharmesh Darshan: (Laughs) Ya Raja Hindustani , which is the Fourth biggest HIT in the History of Indian Cinema.

Priyanka Raina: And Its even Aamir Khan's First Film to have won him the Best Actor, although He was nominated many before that for DIL and Hum hain rahi pyar ke, isn't it?

Dharmesh Darshan: Ya, Its is indeed Aamir Khan's First Filmfare Award & Karisma Kapoor too won the Best Actress. Raja Hindustani won the major Awards and I think became the only film to have all Awards in Major category. Very Few Films had that Combination till date.

Priyanka Raina: Ya Indeed

Dharmesh Darshan: Then Comes MELA, again with Aamir Khan. Then My Romantic and Classic Dhadkan.

Priyanka Raina: DHADKAN, Akshay Kumar whom you have Re launched as an Actor and His image changed totally after that, Comment?

Dharmesh Darshan: No , I don't think so AKSHAY was nothing before then DHADKAN. He has done many Films Before, But Fallen within a Trap, A Trap of Continuously Flop films as there were many Flops in a row . DHADKAN is very difficult for an Action Hero to become a Romantic Hero

Priyanka Raina: Obviously , Akshay was an Action Hero

Dharmesh Darshan: DHADKAN brought him in that Shah Rukh Khan Mode which I would say because I admire Shah Rukh Khan very much...

Priyanka Raina: (Cuts) Cool , We will see Shah Rukh Khan soon with you

Dharmesh Darshan: Ya, DHADKAN had Superb Songs & RAM – The Idol Indian GUY which is still writing for him nicely. But If you give me the Credit, Yes – I take the Credit. But Akshay also worked very hard. He believed in me & allowed me to do the change. Although Suneil Shetty got the Best Supporting Actor Award. The Film also did a lot of Metamorphosis on Shilpa Shetty

Priyanka Raina: And As I think, Shilpa Shetty was nominated for the first Time in Best Actress Category? And it changed the Entire look

Dharmesh Darshan: Yes , Dhadkan Changed the Entire Look and She came out Beautifully upon it. And If you give me the Credit for my Handwork – I will Accept it.

Priyanka Raina: (Laughs) Surely You deserve for bringing up actors out of themselves.

Dharmesh Darshan: (laughs) Thanks & Then after DHADKAN , I did BEWAFA starring Kareena Kapoor.

Priyanka Raina:The Kapoor Sisters, you have worked with Both of them.

Priyanka with Suniel Darshan sir and Karisma Kapoor

Dharmesh Darshan: Yaa , Kapoor Sisters – Kareena and again gave her a very certain Role to look Glamorous In Saree , A Soft Kareena and of coarse with Akshay. And of coarse it was Anil Kapoor, and Sushsmita Sen who seen for the first time ever in Saree.

Priyanka Raina: Yaaa (Laughs)

Dharmesh Darshan: And Then Aap ki Khatir. I had actually suggested **Priyanka Chopra** to my Brother in Andaaz for the second Lead which Raj Kanwar ji Directed it. As they were looking for a girl along with Lara Datta . And I insisted they should check out Priyanka & came out with Priyanka Chopra for you all

Priyanka Raina: And Amisha Patel, She was looking Cute in the movie

Dharmesh Darshan: Amisha Patel was there in a small Role , But was a pleasure working with her. And Even I enjoyed working with Akshaye Khanna – He is a Very good Actor indeed

Priyanka Raina: And Dino Morya, who was CON guy

Dharmesh Darshan: Yes, Sunil Shetty, Anupam Kher , Dino – There were so many people But **Akshaye** was a Fantastic Person. I had been very fortunate that way, and worked with very good Actors

Priyanka Raina: And Whom we call Mr. Perfectionist AAMIR KHAN has done two films with you, as He does not do the second film with anyone, Correct?

Dharmesh Darshan: Yes, Aamir has done two films with me. The Reason Aamir doesn't do second film with anyone, because **his Style is actually mine..... (laughs) I do one film everyone.**

Priyanka Raina: So Now when we are seeing Next DHARMESH DHARSHAN film back on screen?

Dharmesh Darshan: People are confused, that I have taken a Break for last Five years. After 2007 , I didn't Direct any film. But If you see- Raja Hindustani and Dhadkan too had a Gap of Five years

Sanjay suri, Dharmesh Darshan and Priyanka Raina

Priyanka Raina: Oh ! Five Golden Years.... So That means we will see you soon on Screens

Dharmesh Darshan: Hopefully, something as good as Dhadkan, and also There are lots of reasons for taking this gap of FIVE years. I lost my Both parents – 2009 My Mother and Last year , Lost my Dad.

Priyanka Raina: Oh ! I am so sorry.

Dharmesh Darshan: So I was not in a mood to make films. But I think since last films Directors are not getting that importance. It is the just STAR value. And I am used to not Bigger then the star but Equal then Star . But I feel that , when Director has no value – Achievers Directors like me has to work hard upon movies

Priyanka Raina: Noo, But in Today's Cinema even KARAN JOHAR is Director who is equal to the star.

Dharmesh Darshan: Yes , But Karan Johar is a Producer/ Director. I am just a Director – A Free Lancer Director.

Priyanka Raina: So See you very soon, Firing on BOX OFFICE.

Dharmesh Darshan: See, I am a kind of Guy who can end up with Three films in one year or One Film in Three Years. But it should be a Good Film with Good Story. I do a project , which has Respect, Values, Our Indian Culture.

Priyanka Raina: And you will do a project with Newcomers or with Stars?

Dharmesh Darshan: I can work with anyone. If you notice my career , I worked with everyone. I have worked with under dogs

Priyanka Raina: Exactly, you are the who has made actors- And they won their First Filmfare Trophies from your movie.

Dharmesh Darshan: I don't believe (laughs) . I always dis what I feel like and automatically you should be a little marketable for you Producers- And every producer of mine in Six Films weather it is Ratan Jain ji, Boney Kapoor Sahab, TIPS, Cineyug have earned HUGE profits out of it. I have done two to three films with each of them & they always repeated it.

Priyanka Raina: Dharmesh ji, You are known for the Longest KISS in the History of Indian Film Industry & which I think Till today it's the only movie which is played , where we don't change our Channels as Rest Channels are changed

Dharmesh Darshan: See, I can't say about any other Directors But can certainly speak about myself. See, Kiss is very Reflective & I believe in Human emotions weather it is sensuality. I don't shy away from it. But it has to be neatly done. It should be beautiful & no audience should be isolated with it. As it was a very daring statement to shoot a Kiss

Priyanka Raina: Obviously.....

Dharmesh Darshan: But as you say, no body shifts the channel after seeing this particular scene & Karisma's image became even better, Aamir 's image too became even better. So lots of thought keep coming & perhaps I believe – I am the idol member in the Industry , I guess (Laughs)

Priyanka Raina: Why have you been so Publicity shy and not taken the credit for building in so many Actors Tenure in a day where each and everyone makes a noise of every Bit of it ?

Dharmesh Darshan: I believe "GOD CREATES". I had never been a Video Maniac. Yes my Effort was very much , and as I strongly believe, Nobody can give you that recognition which GOD can give you. Yes, sometimes I do feel hurt when people who have climbed up my shoulders and have totally Denied me – Forget , giving me the credit. But I think , I had never made a noise about it. I began with grace, Did my work & if anyone's career Build up – Its Great and will Pray to God "It should build up"

Priyanka Raina: Great & Since you Media shy, For the first time – Thanks for speaking with us on our Official Channel.

Dharmesh Darshan: (Laughs) Its not the first time, But one of the rare times. You are a very Sweet Girl & you write very Positively about everybody weather it is interview or Film Reviews. I personally had gone through all your Blogs.

Priyanka Raina: Thank you

Priyanka Raina photographed by Dharmesh Darshan sir

Dharmesh Darshan: That's a very fresh perspective in the Media & Healthy. And I want to encourage this Healthy behavior. I have lots of friends in the media, But you know Priyanka – I am a Person who has never manipulated the Media. I have never played with the media. I have genuinely respected the Media.

Priyanka Raina: Exactly, you had never been in news for any controversy.

Dharmesh Darshan: But Yes I Think , It's the Time to ask for Credit. Because In today, We can't Command, until we Demand upon it; Right?

Yes , Exacltly & that was the One of the most SEASONED Director "DHARMESH DARSHAN"

CHAPTER TWELVE

Interviews Meet and Interview with Manoj Bajpayee

Manoj Bajpai in Recent conversation with Priyanka Raina clarifies about his Acting oriented Roles as he talks about his forth coming Film TEVAR

Priyanka Raina : Tell me something about your Role in TEVAR , because till now as you have a record that you chose Acting oriented film instead of commercial film

Manoj Bajpai : I don't go for commercial film because I find myself into one craft. I don't just want to do Commercial just for the sake of money or just being part of it. I do a film if the Role is good , Character Oriented , Gives a lot of scope or if it will have possibility of becoming a great one

Priyanka Raina : You have been part of Film Industry with biggest ever Director Yash Chopra , Like when Yash approached you for Veer Zaara - What made you choose over the Role

Manoj Bajpai : Yash ji , Yash ji and only Yash ji. Because Yash ji (Yash Chopra) is someone that we all admired since Childhood , we had grown up watching his films , and like everyone had a dream to be part of his creation. so even if offer coming from him just for Guest Appearance - and for a while just to be Directed by Him anyone will say Yes. And That's only the reason I choose and we maintained a very good Relationship with each other , A good Bounding with Yash Chopra

Priyanka Raina : you have done a few commercial films like Gangs of Wassaipur....

Manoj Bajpai : Never , I have never done a commercial film in my life and will never do . I am a theater Artist and respect Work . I do Roles that give certain message to public.

Priyanka Raina : You choose roles over Political Satire , so even your character in TEVAR is related to it?

Manoj Bajpai: I don't do roles over Political Satire . And my character in TEVAR is equally important as he is after girl but she doesn't wants to be with him. In one way , you can call it a parallel love story

Priyanka Raina : Recently Sonakshi Tweeted about Arjun Kapoor , "Saale ke TEVAR t dekho , Mujhe chod kar BIG BOSS Mein chala gaya " your comment on this

Manoj Bajpai : (Laughs) Arjun Kapoor went their to promote song of film . and recently EROS told all three of us to come for Promotions and we came . Today they told just me , So am here.

Priyanka Raina : The Last Word- As Film Name is TEVAR.... Who has shown most TEVAR in shooting

Manoj Bajpai : (Laughs) One and only Arjun Kapoor . Further Tells , but Arjun is very good and spontaneous Actor and he has a great ability to learn new things.

Manoj Bajpayee, Priyanka Raina

Also Interviews are available online on Priyanka Raina 's Official website www.themagicpr.com and www.priyankaraina.co.in

CHAPTER THIRTEEN

Meet and Interview with Sanjay Kapoor

Bollywood Film Actor turned Recently Producer with his very first movie "TEVAR" **Sanjay Kapoor** in interaction with **Priyanka Raina** says , "To turn Film Producers are I think in our jeans. My Dad was a Producer, Boney was too, Rhea too entered in Production , Even my Brother Anil Kapoor turned Producer and so Here I am " SO here we go Film Production are in our jeans.

Priyanka Raina : Who was having the most TEVAR while shooting the film

Sanjay Kapoor : The person who was having the most TEVAR was our film ,which was more important for us. Our Story , our faith in that , and that's the reason it is shown on screen with some Good work
Our Film TEVAR has lots of Tevar and needed to be well guided. That's the reason We have taken a Fresh Director Amit Sharma , who has Directed over 400 Ad Films.

Priyanka Raina : So firstly story was written , and Director came into picture. I mean the concept is your's.....

Sanjay Kapoor : No , not exactly. We thought of making on such a subject, but when we signed Director then the story was rewritten according to him and that's how you will see it further.

Priyanka Raina : Can we say say TEVAR as typical Masala film or Love Triangle as Manoj bajpai said in his recent interview

Sanjay Kapoor : Sometimes we can say Interpretation of the writer may be wrong. Like we have shown in our Trailer , its not just a Masala film but its beyond that. Yes TEVAR is a Lover triangle shot on outskirts of Agra and Mathura.

We have taken a Fresh Director who has his name in AD World . We have taken fresh casting , Sonakshi Sinha and Arjun Kapoor are coming for the first time. Even a Negative character is important for us , because with charm of Negative Positive won't get its impact. TEVAR is basically a Romantic film.

Further **Sanjay Kapoor** Adds , "I want to thank to the Government of Agra and Mathura for supporting us . We have shot the film on Live locations so that u can feel the environment:

Sanjay Kapoor, Priyanka Raina

Also Interviews are available online on Priyanka Raina 's Official website www.themagicpr.com and www.priyankaraina.co.in

CHAPTER FOURTEEN

Meet and Interview with Rani Mukerji

Rani Mukerji Chopra formally known as "Queen of Hearts" of Millions around there, Now guesses formally will be known for "Queen of Sequels" (Jokes apart)....

From playing a character who was affected by **Tourette syndrome** in **HICHKI** to a powerful Cop in **Mardaani 2** , **Rani Mukerji** proudly says to **Priyanka Raina** "For shooting , I have to leave my Baby and come. So I ensure that films I choose are more driven towards society"

"Rapes is something that disturbs a Women inside you, For example if women is watching on TV at Home and we probably change the channel as it disturbs. But I think its the time to speak against it and work on it. As we are Filmmakers , so I choose Films as a medium to say my word" **Rani Mukerji** continues.

And **SELF DEFENCE** or Martial Arts is necessity , that I think every girl or Boy should learn for theor own safety.

Also continuing **As Mardaani had a sequel on its success and even HICHKI is powerful Hit** , So will us be seeing **HICHKI 2** ? On this Rani Mukerji says (With Laughs) "Why not , Now I will be probably called as Sequel queen.

Rani Mukerji , Priyanka Raina

Well to add on , **Rani Mukherji** at a moment is more fascinated towards Content Driven films , and **Adira** loves singing and dancing so may will doing a light comedy film next where **Adira** can probably enjoy the mode in.

CHAPTER FIFTEEN

Meet and Interview with Ekta Kapoor

"Ajeeb Dastaan Hai Yeh" is an unusual heart warming story of two strangers Shobha & Vikram who meet each other by stroke of Luck and get bounded by a String of Unusual Relationship.

Ekta Kapoor speaks to **Priyanka Raina** about using titles **"Ajeeb Dastaan Hai Yeh"** , **"Bade Achche Lagte Hain"** Titles over famous Epics songs, on how it helps to get over it. Watch Chat Exclusively in Video

Sonali Bendre to make a Television Fiction Debut with the Show opposite **Apoorva Agnihotri** .

"Ajeeb Dastaan Hai Yeh" is an **Balaji Telefilms** Presentation.

Also Priyanka Raina started her acting with "Balaji Telefilms" playing a small role in Kyunki Saas bhi kabhi bahu thi

Ekta Kapoor , Priyanka Raina

Interviews are available online on Priyanka Raina 's Official website www.themagicpr.com and www.priyankaraina.co.in

Actor/ Director Priyanka Raina meets with the Entire Bhatt Camp to Celebrate the Success of RAAZ 3, as it the First Expensive film in the Bhatt Camp & First 3D film. "First of all, Let me Congratulate on the phenomenal success of RAAZ 3 and Although the 3D is Brilliant, What Gave you the idea to make this film on 3D, when previous films were on 2D ?", As asked By Priyanka

Mahesh Bhatt, Priyanka Raina

Mahesh Bhatt Says, "We just thought about 3D , because we wanted the entire Theater to part of us. We wanted that feel to come within them, so they can see the Ghost, and that's all. It was just a Small try and rest is all on Public. They Liked Concept."

Priyanka Raina : "Oh Yes, and some scenes really made us scared, and especially that Cockroach one, could feel as if they are in theater. At one instinct , I removed my goggles to see - oh they are in movie. He He"

Mahesh Bhatt : "Oh Yeah, That scene is Highlight of the movie & it has been Shot beautifully. "Mukesh Bhatt: "First of all, Let Me congratulate that your reviews are well written. And RAAZ 3 is a special film in every way- First 3D film, First Expensive Film and But at the End , It has to be liked by Viewers. And Thanks everyone for Appreciating our Movie.

Bipasha Basu , Priyanka Raina

Ofcoarse, It is Well Made Film and It has to be appreciated. And So Here it is, Chat with the Entire Bhatt camp. It was fabulas meeting the Legends of the Industry. Read RAAZ 3 Review Complete By Priyanka Raina

Also Mahesh Bhatt is Director of Hum hain rahi pyar ke

CHAPTER SEVENTEEN

From **Chote Nawab** to **Bullet Raja**, Here comes our Saif Ali Khan speaking exclusively to Priyanka Raina in JW MARRIOT, Juhu. **Saif Ali Khan** speaks about **Manoj Kumar** Roles

Priyanka Raina: Till now, you had a lot of varieties in your Role weather it is **OLE OLE** or **OMKARA**, If ever a Patriotic script is offered to you - Will you do it?

Saif Ali Khan : I like Variations , But if you are a Patriotic only one thing comes to my mind "**MANOJ KUMAR**". Yaa But its has to be Modernized according to today's era & most important it has be Commercialized. Movie should Entertain Audience.

    Priyanka Raina : What do you look in Script, Before signing?

Saif Ali Khan : I see , if it is Entertaining myself or not?

Well Chote Nawab , you are truly a Rockstar & keep doing Good Stuff

Saif ali khan, Priyanka Raina

Interviews are available online on Priyanka Raina 's Official website www.themagicpr.com and www.priyankaraina.co.in

CHAPTER EIGHTEEN

Meet and Interview with Satish Kaushik, Gauri Shinde

<u>"Cinema is nit Glamorous , But it's a profession we have to be proud of"</u>

When Reliance Entertainment Backed out from Prestigious Film Fest MAMI This year , How the Entire Industry came in support and to make our "Mumbai Film Festival" happen This year. Well **Priyanka Raina** Talks Exclusively about MAMI to **Rajeev Masand** (Film Critic) , **Satish Kaushik** (Director) , **Gauri Shinde** (Director).

Priyanka Raina tells , "Almost after major one backing out we thought the festival was not going to happen. But This time instead of COOPERATES , Entire Film Industry came ahead to support MAMI which altogether is Unique thing. Thats why this festival is important then all previous years "

Rajeev Masand Further says , "If Film Lovers and Film Industry did not get up to give their support , I think this we could not make it happen"

Gauri Shinde , " Its such a good a thing that without any discussion everyone just came in together. "

Satish Kaushik , " I have been attending MAMI for four to five years in past but this time it was important for me as have fallen in JURY section which itself is a very great section. It for Youth , It's for People who are interested in Cinema. It is important , it was started by Jaya bachchan and we are are getting so many good films. How many films are this year (68 , said by Priyanka) so out of 68 good films , we have shortlisted 20 which we are going to see. Cinemaa is seeking into people as profession

Satish Kaushik , Priyanka Raina

Priyanka Raina : What you would say about Festival happening this year just for seven Days?

Priyanka Raina: Seven Days.... I would say Seven good days of our lovely Film Industry, Lots of good film happening

Gauri Shinde : It was disappointing for almost all of us that this year festival may not happen , But everyone came together Film Industry , Film Lovers and Your festival is here"

Satish Kaushik : As part of JURY is a great Dimension , and These seven days are itself are biggest dimension, Best days of our lives when Entire Film Industry is together under one roof. and Biggest thing is that International Film Market and Our Film Industry meets.

Priyanka Raina : And One Last Important Question , Goa Film Festival which is happening since years on only 300 & MAMI fees are increasing every year. Do you think think is that the cause for Loss?

Rajeev Masand : Goa Film Festival is Government festival and funds are organised by Government. Government has losts of funds and MAMI is a private festival. But unique thing is that inspite of this Film Lovers are coming and we are getting good response.

Gauri Shinde : Oh is that so , well I was not aware what are fees. How much is it (1600 , Told By Priyanka). Oh I don't think that is the reason. MAMI is a Private festival and if you are a real Film lover you will borrow money anyhow and attend your festival & People are watching movies in multiplexes and spending 1000's . Here even then are getting many good film. And inspite of that we are getting good response this year

Satish Kaushik : No its not that . If you taking festival as Money making machine , then you are going wrong. And money wise , they are so many new comers that they are losing money in so many things , That way Festival is beneficial for them - they are learning so many things.

Priyanka Raina : And My self even I am a Film maker , I have Directed Seven short film till date, Assisted in feature films & It all started with MAMI. I was attending MAMI since 2010 thats when I made my first short film in these four wonderful years. Got many good friends from MAMI

Satish Kaushik : I know , I have seen you at MAMI . One such good thing is that , even if film makers are not capable of budget wise. They any how arrange and Yes they create a story and shoot a film from mobile camera or Handycam , make it happen like a International film

Priyanka Raina : Even I made SEVEN short films till date, **Clean and Green India** & latest one being **ZINDAGI**

Satish Kaushik : See now That's call Passion for cinema, If you have the will to do, you can do anything in life you shoot on Handycam or %D but you do it. And Being a Film maker my self, we get to see so many films across . Dimension is a great platform for these Young Film Filmmakers and one sitting write in front of me.

"Cinema is not a Glamourous , But its a Profession that we have to be proud of it" , Satish Kaushik Adds

CHAPTER NINETEEN

Meet and Interview with "Filmistan" Team

Filmistan [Jisse Filmo se ho pyaar , wo Filmistan se kaise kare Inkaar]
Filmistan , which ia indeed a **Tribute to Bollywood** with all the punchlines of Hit films on 1970s of Mega star **Amitabh Bachchan**. Directed by Nitin Kakkad , Here comes our **Filmstan** cast **Sharib Hashmi** and **InaamUlHaq** chatting Exclusively to Priyanka Raina. Also Sharib Hashmi had acted before in **Jab Tak Hai Jaan** before , Directed by Yash Chopra.

Sharib Hanshmi, Priyanka Raina, InamUlHaq

Priyanka Raina : When ever a Film comes on "Hindustan and Pakistan", It has always been appreciated weather its is a Film Like BORDER or Cricket Match.

Inaamulhaq : When ever Film comes on Hindustan and Pakistan, it had always been appreciated. Not only that Indian films are loved across the Borders. All the Indian Stars have huge fan following across the Borders

Priyanka Raina : Not only that, even Pakistani Actors and Actress that have come to Bollywood have got huge following

Inaamulhaq : yaa Actors like Meera , **Zara Shaikh** , **Veena** and even **Ali Zafar** are doing great. There 's a huge conflict , which I think we can change by our films. and by making Films on "Hindustan and Pakistan" we can Bring the Love Back.How much Love we get in Hindustan , that much only we get in Pakistan. "Hindustan and Pakistan" are two different countries on Globe, but in deep they are one only.

Priyanka Raina : So In this film , there are different punchlines of Amitabh Bachchan Sir which are said by you. So how honoured you felt and what was your observation while saying in Amitabh Bachchan style,

Sharib Hashmi : Means , when we saying Amitabh Bachchan sir dialogues in his style , It was a different feeling in all and was totally fun.And through this Film , how FILMIPAN was within us everything we put on screen.

Priyanka Raina: Full Filmistan

Sharib Hashmi and Inaamulhaq : Jai ho Cinema ki....

Sharib Hashmi : and as you said , Films combine two nations. and in cricket its is always My team and your team where as Film always unite watch by Both nations together. **Films are very big Support which keeps us together, which we said by medium of FILMISTAN**

InaamUlHaq , Priyanka Raina , Pankaj Udhas and Sharib Hanshmi

Priyanka Raina : So one last Punchline , which you would like to say for Filmistan

Sharib Hashmi and Inaamulhaq : Jisse Filmo se ho pyaar , wo Filmistan se kaise kare Inkaar

CHAPTER TWENTY

Meet and Interview with Puneet Issar

God is Being Kind to Me – Puneet Issar in conversation with Priyanka Raina

An Actor who has given "n" Number of Performances weather its Negative character in Zakhmi Aurat or Patriotic Soldier in BORDER or ELLAN E JUNG. Apart from Acting ,in Direction also given one of the Super hits Movie **GARV Starring Salman Khan.** A Man who almost needs no description , A Legend , A Versatile Actor or Duryodhana of BR Chopra's Epic MAHABHARATA - PUNEET ISSAR speaking about his journey to Priyanka Raina on the Glorious Republic Day

Priyanka Raina : A Legend who has played iconic Roles in Epic MAHABHARATA in late 80s when Roads used to almost get empty on telecast of serial. So tell us something about memories associated with Chopra's , Your Collaboration with them?

Puneet Issar : I would like to say that Shri BR Chopra Sahab and Ravi Chopra who created Mahabharata which could be redefined as one of EPICS. I believe myself luckier enough to be blessed with a Divine Grand DURYODHANA so that I could become part of his iconic character. My association with Ravi Chopra ji is being eligible as I got an opportunity to play an Iconic character of DURYODHANA which was loved and appreciated by everyone inspite of its negative shades.

Puneet Issar, Priyanka Raina

Priyanka Raina : MAHABHARATA - First Grand Serial to be Aired on DOORDARSHAN and when it was screened Roads usually used to get empty . How were your feelings at that time?

Puneet Issar : मेरा भ्शेक यह मानना है कि अच्छी फिल्में बनती नही दरसल इशवर उन्हें बना देता है। Every Actor and Director works very hard,But its God's Destiny अच्छी फिल्में बनाइ नही ंजाती ; बन जाती है I

Priyanka Raina : Also you have acted in Feature Films portraying Different characters weather its Patriotic (RATAN SINGH) in BORDER or Negative one of ZAKHMI AURAT Directed By Avtar Bhogal or the one in ELLAN E

JUNG By Anil Sharma. All Characters played by you are with full Dedication and energy

Puneet Issar : देखिए, मैं एक कलाकार हूँ। I am a Trained Myth Actor. I had been a Professor in Acting Classes, So as a result use to teach Diction, Improvisation, etc. A Role is a Role, doesn't mind weather negative or Positive. It shows your versatility to be a good Actor. So what ever Role you get, Do with your full dedication and energy. मैनें जो भी करिदार कयिा हैं, मैनें उस करिदार को जयिा हो weather its RATAN SINGH or Main Villain of Zakhmi Aurat.

Priyanka Raina : Apart from Acting , Even In Direction you had been versatile with Superhits Creations like GARV starring SuperStar Heartthrob Salman Khan !

Puneet Issar : I am Writer/Director of GARV & I consider myself Lucky to have given SUPERHIT with SuperStar Salman Khan. It was Honor to Direct SALMAN KHAN which needs almost no description. Also in year 1995, I had Directed Serial called HINDUSTANI which was Super Hit and was Aired on channel for continuously Three Years. Then I made another serial JAI MATA KI featuring Hema Malini, where Hema ji had played all characters of DEVI's including Durga, Saraswati, Lakshmi - which was again Super Hit and loved by all.

Priyanka Raina : (Laughs) I have seen GARV in theaters Three Times, that too after bunking my college. We used to got just for Salman Khan.

Puneet Issar : I have made Two serials which were Super Hits and proved to be longest running serials at late 90s. Then I had made GARV which was again Mega HIT. I actually believe "GOD IS Being KIND TO ME" Salman is like my younger brother and mostly by love he calls me PUNS which in BIG BOSS by calling PUNS he has made an Eye catcher for viewers. Now wherever I go even Small Child calls me "PUNS, How are you". Salman has made me Popular by PUNS not only in India , But in Entire World. So I believe that After BIG BOSS Puneet Issar got a New Birth of PUNS.

Priyanka Raina : Well , PUNS is new name of Puneet ji !

Puneet Issar : (Laughs) And even I want to clarify one thing that my friendship with Salman is 35 years older and He calls me Big Brother which he had also said on National Television

Priyanka Raina : Big Boss Journey had many ups and Downs in you life , Like at one moment you were kept out of Home. what were your feelings at time ?

Puneet Issar : When a person goes to Big Boss Home, He makes himself mentally prepared to perform the tasks given. Whenever you loose,Its obvious you will be punished. I had gone to BIG BOSS Home with my full belief that I will not say any bad words to Women nor will abuse them nor am going to use my strength against Women. Because of this , I had lost Tasks n Number of times and was punished too.

Priyanka Raina : Exactly you had never used your strength against anyone & many times you were not even participating in Tasks

Puneet Issar : I was sure that "मैं बल का प्रयोग नहीं करूंगा" & with staying in my limits, I had played Game with full energy. And overall its a Big thing That I had Stayed for 15 Weeks in BIG BOSS home which in all is a Record for any 40+ Actors. In which I was nominated for Thirteen Weeks but I never crossed my limits to be safe. I had slept on floors, been outside the home

Priyanka Raina : You were sleeping on Floors , infact P3G group was sleeping and they had made there best comfort place near SOFA

Puneet Issar : As there's a Saying , "When going gets tough, Tough gets going". So we were tough enough इसी बहाने एक सयम आया ; कठोर परक्षिम कयिा और अपने आप को बगि के घर में पाया और बहुत कछु सखिा है बगि बोस से

Priyanka Raina : Your Relation with Arya Babbar in Big Boss home was not good after that incident happened. I am asking this , because I am Acting student from EKJUTE and have done plays with him. Although Arya was wrong in that task , what you would like to comment on this?

Puneet Issar : Would like say about Arya Babbar one thing, First of all his Dad (Raj Babbar) is my Senior. My Dad had made one film called PREM

GEET , A Super Hit film which was the Introduction of Raj Babbar in Bollywood. In that one song was there, if you remember होंटो से छूलो तुम; मेरे गीत अमर कर दो . So Raj Babbar comes in our very old family relation and Arya Babbar is just like my younger brother. Whatever has happened, was during one task where undoubtedly I had used strength but it was not knowingly. After that We have hugged each other and said sorry.Arya was my younger brother and will always be, and I will always pray that he what ever he does in his life, He gets success and Arya He has written a book and I wish him all the luck for it

Priyanka Raina : What is the secret of your energy?

Puneet Issar : I had seen that maximum 40+ who come in Big Boss home like Navjot Singh Sidhu or Ismail Darbaar , maximum bound to stay for merely three to four weeks. I am 55 years old and stayed for 105 days and not only this who are half the age of mine, I am more Fit and strong then them because I workout for Six hours a Day. Infact after going in Big Boss , I had lost 18 kilos of weight.

Priyanka Raina : Would you Like to work with Salman Khan again?

Puneet Issar : Of Course I am making a film on life of Gama Pehlwan under Salman Khan Production called GAMA. He was one of the Pahelwaans of India in Ancient Times, Dedicated on his life am making a Film GAMA

Priyanka Raina : And PUNS the Last Word.........

Puneet Issar : Its new Birth of PUNS. I am 56 years but people consider me as 24 years old , and even I don't want to grow beyond that. Even I have taken the stay order, and PUNS will always stay 24 year old Kid (Laughs)

AtMahabharata Play with Puneet Issar and Jyothi Venkatesh

When we talk about the Epic serial "MAHABHARATA" – What comes in our minds. The serial which created History on Doordarshan, The Serial which brought whole everyone in front of Television, The Serial which emptied out the roads , and lots more....

Epic Serial by BR CHOPRA films , Directed by Ravi Chopra was one of the biggest ever first serial which reached miles.

One character of Mahabharata which was important on its terms , That would get smile on face is KRISHNA played by Nitish Bharadwaj . From Gokul ki Masti to Kans Vadh to creating a new city DWARKA to HASTINAPUR – Every journey tells a Unique story.

Priyanka Raina, Nitish Bharadwaj and Rakesh Bedi

Also the Key factor Siddhant Issar who Debuts in Acting as Young Daryodhan has given a Brilliant performance and not only acting , He had also written Dialogues along with Puneet Issar and Team.

Siddhant Issar , PriyankavRaina and Puneet Issar

Interviews are available online on Priyanka Raina 's Official website www.themagicpr.com and www.priyankaraina.co.in

CHAPTER TWENTY-ONE

Meet and Interview with Dharmendra

Only Salman Khan can play my biopic- Dharmendra in Exclusive to Priyanka Raina

Talking to Legend, Icon , You need almost no words to define a divine Tycoon Personality- Bollywood Superstar **Dharmendra** (mostly known as Dharam Paaji by love).

It was a Fun Frolic loving chat session with Dharam ji , as chatting on his upcoming movie "Second Hand Husband". Also Dharam ji told, That my character is very much fun loving and very much identifies my Real life story.

Dharmendra, Priyanka Raina

Also asked that "If either a story is made on ur Autobiography or Biopic, which Actor you would like to play your Role". Dharam ji said, "It will be one and only Salman Khan as resembles very much me. We Both have same habits (Laughs)"

Also on asking on his health issues , on his recent Shoulder injury - Dharam ji replied "Yes I am very mush fine, actually while I was shooting I just fell down and I started laughing and as a result everyone started laughing. And then went to Doctor there was small injury and I thought to do compete check up and that's it. For safety"

Then asked like What are you Taking your Safety precautions , Dharam ji said "Bas Khaane peene ka parhez hai".

On this I laughingly told , Khaane ka ya peene ka. Dharam ji laughingly replied "Last quote is much better".

Also Dharam Paaji reveals formula of staying young and energetic forever , that Keep smiling and be a good Human ,helping other- you will always remain Sweet 16.

Well ,Bollywood Gharam Dharma success Mantra is so sweet, keep smiling and always cheering others. Wishing you Best wishes with Second hand husband.

CHAPTER TWENTY-TWO

Meet and Interview with Esha Deol

Talking to Esha Deol was always special as she ha just acted in Short film. As myself am a short film maker, I always promote Short film. "According to me films are not small or Big. Films are defined by its good content" -Priyanka Raina gets Exclusive with Esha Deol

Esha Deol – The Original Dhoom girl got married to her Childhood friend **Bharat Takhtani** which is truly a **Cakewalk** journey for her to cherish upon. Chill ! Cakewalk is is not only her comeback short film But also opens a platform for Short film makers to Release on **Rishtey Cineplex** , Directed by **Ram Kamal Mukherjee** .

"Firstly , Esha Deol s favourite films of all times is Na Tum Jaano Hum which is my favorite too " **Priyanka Raina** adds.

Ram Kamal Mukerji, Esha Deol and Priyanka Raina

Now Coming to Esha Deol 's Experience on working with Debutant Director **Ram Kamal Mukherjee** , She adds "Ram is a wonderful person who comes out with his full homework. They didnt make me feel at all that it was set, Felt just like a Home"

Also **Esha Deol 's message to the youth on Short Films**, "Life is truly a Cakewalk , and its wonderful that **Colors CEO Raj Nayak** is coming with special edition for Short films makers with some thing like this – Where even 20 Min Short film gets a Bigger platform

Apart interviewing Actors , Filmmaking is something that you discover youself, Get new ideas in life when you meet people. In short Filmmaking is all about travels. So post end of 2014 started discovering places and first solo Trip was paradise on Earth – Kashmir.

Kashmir

As a filmmaker, you have to be your best friend, Love yourself, Talk to yourself. Here's how you develop a story. Something to get excited upon. As flight landed in Kashmir, Announcement made "Please wear your jackets, Temperature is -1 outside".

I was pretty nervous as never been in cold city, was thinking what if I fell ill. Thinking and was walking towards the door. When doors opened, cool breeze came which smile on my face. I said "Oh wow Natural Air condition" and walked out.

Next day while I was taking a Shikara Ride to Char minar which is situated within the waters, Could feel the politeness within me. So calm and peace that you can hear the sound of Waters.

Also was singing song from Mission Kashmir , **Chupke se sun Is pal ki dhun** to the waters. Kashmir s indeed paradise on earth.

Shikara Ride

Beauty of Kashmir cant be compared to anyone in this world ; where can ride Boat in DUL LAKE or enjoy the most enchanting places in GULMARG with full of snow. Gulmarg has lots of more activities like mountain climbing ; Ice Skeeing; Cable Cars and lots more. Also can enjoy the lovely Kashmiri food and Black tea known as Kashmiri Kawa , Things to Do in Kashmir , Ice Ski , Cycle.

Discovered many places in world as Switzerland next stop. Who don't love to be in mountains, A road which is free from pollution for cycling, jogging – That could be another Dream destination for holidaying, isn't it?

So Let me tell something about Leukerbad , A small village situated in Suburbs of Switzerland and 30 minutes away from Leuk Station.

Zurich

This can be one of the Dream destinations for shootings, filming a dream sequence as surrounded by Mountains, Ice skating and also Cable cars.

Population of Leukerbad may be around 1590 and area would be 67.2 kms square. Also one can see Cows eating grass in fiends with no man guarding on them. Instead they are put with Sim in their neck, in case if they get lost – One can locate them through Mobile data.

Well now apart from this, also Leukerbad has MIGROS which has all the eatables stuff, Clothes and daily requirements for living. And PIZZERIA , A hang out chilling place for youngsters

Apart from this , Leukerbad also has a Gym where people can come for Fitness. Gym is situated with Mountain hiking's, Lawn Tennis, Basket Ball and so on games.

As we all work into our Busy schedules , so it gets more important to take out for yourself and be in the world of Dreamland. Arrived in Budapest as of Holidays after taking a Break from my next writing of a movie , and falling in love with its amazing weather at 3 degrees Temperature.

Just as we stepped in to see to the Statue situated on the Top of Hill , located after crossing 1000 stairs and View of the city is wonderful from there .

Now coming to The Statue view situated 20 mins walk from Corvin city at Budapest. Its in the Top of hill from where can view the entire BUDAPEST

Budapest parliament

Also Its lovely to shoot a song sequence in the total Dreamland like "**Yeh Kahan aa gaye Hum**" and many more to talk on.

In Budapest places like Budapest parliament carved in Gold , Budapest castles are the best places to hang around. Also the Cruise Dinner is the highlight of the day.

Dubai is a place have been more than 10 times, every time travel here just feels like still refreshing. Dubai Marina Festival 2016 of Arts & Theaters is a festival happening for a wee in Dubai, with lots of performances in Singing , Puppet Show & many more !

Dubai

Dubai Marina Festival 2016 is basically a street festival, that is held in surroundings of Marina lake with some lovely performances. Its like Another city in world, which tells a lot about itself – A place which has no religion (People from India, US, UK, Pakistan, Afghanistan & many more staying under one roof) . Besides, It has Metros , Biggest malls, Bruj Khalifa,

Tallest Buildings, TRAMS , Beaches, Desserts & lots more . In short , A sweet cocktail !!

Travelling continued with **Manali** Adventure and believe if you have not been to manali, Just have to be here once in a life time. There's lots to do here, Like whenever films are based on Travels, We filmmakers research a lot.

Like in my recent interview with Director **Siddharth Anand** who is known for Travels making, When I asked **"How do you manage getting the locations perfect framed that goes with your characters"**

Siddharth Anand , Priyanka Raina

On this Siddharth Anand opens up that I treat my Locations as a Character in the film. I try and give my audience experience while sitting in the theater that they see the world. And if they see some locations that they haven't seen it before, Then indefinitely they ask me that **where Did you shoot that scene or song**? Then they decide to go there. This is something which I want to carry forward, Not many Directors in India are able to capture or showcase locations like which are a Treat to the eyes. **Showcase your locations well, Treat it as one of your characters**, "Give it importance s that is why People question me that I make films on Travels, That is my intent to showcase the world" Siddharth says with Exclamation.

Coming to **Priyanka Raina** on **Manali** LOcations visit, "Manali is one of the Incredible Hill stations situated in the Himalayas"

How to reach Manali – To come to **Manali** , Its either way you go on a road Trip from CHANDIGARH which is 4 Hours 45 mins journey. Like I came from Chandigarh Airport to KULU Airport. Thrilled to see, KULU AIRPORT is a beautiful and small Airport on a HILL STATION.

MAnali resort

Then From **KULU Airport** to reach **OLD MANALI** is actually 55 KMS away which may take around 2 hours, so decided to see some locations on the way, as coming again travelling for hours would take time.

First been to this SHAWL factory where **Shimla** based shawl are created , Handcrafted shawls . It was lovely interacting with locals there on "How shawls are created, Real **SUI DHAAGA** ones "

Then coming to RIVER RAFTING , which was 15 minutes away from KULLU AIRPORT, so thought of Discovering on how we experience siting in rides Believe me, its fun and scary too But I think that's what we call it as "Adventurous", Isn't It?

Put on our Life jackets and Helmets , took the boats down through a CURVE that connected Road to water straight. And then ready to rock and roll for a complete hilarious ride

Well there are lots more which will be coming shortly, till then don't forget to follow our blog to get complete details on **INCREDIBLE INDIA**.

Even the south unlike Bangalore, Hyderabad are one of the Exciting places. Bangalore was there for shooting a south film and had a Hyderabad visit as had work in Ramoji filmcity

Ramoji film city

Well there's lots to tell about city with its beautiful carvings and CHAR MINAR, till then we come to beautiful memories of Bangalore city which has given me opportunity to work in South film.

Here we go , the word 'Travel' makes you just with youself. Travelling Amritsar, Chandigarh and Rajasthan. Rajasthan has memories as went there for Film festival. It had a screening for a friend Monjoy Mukerji's Hai apna dil to awara. So while tour of city thought of an idea "Guy cheating upon Two girls" or also can be vice versa

Sheesh mahal

Discussed its with Monjoy, He like the idea and so helped me in writing its screenplay. That's how my Short film **Love Lust Locha** happened as we were discussing story that Two girls falling for the same Guy , But that was in 90s. Now would be complete Locha. And then we began the auditions at

Filmalaya studio for LOVE LUST LOCHA which is now airing at Sony Liv

CHAPTER TWENTY-FOUR

Interviews with Vaani Kapoor and Siddharth Anand

Debuting from **Shudh Desi Romance** to Being the coolest **Befikre** Girl landing up on **WAR,** Vaani Kapoor has huge love for Travel films. And Unlike **Siddharth Anand** does films on Travel so well weather its Salaam Namaste or Now WAR.

"There's a certain Graph to the character that I am Portraying , and As **WAR** is Action based on these Two Super Heroes (**Tiger Shroff** and **Hrithik Roshan**)- There's a lot of story , Hopefully everybody will discover" , **Vaani Kapoor** Kick starts the **WAR** with **Priyanka Raina**.

Vaani Kapoor, Priyanka Raina

Getting **WAR** is being tough , As you have got through a long system of Auditions and that's how YRF system is . For every actor you have to Audition for the role . Shanoo Sharma is being supportive and have being guiding to get through my audition round.

Also I love Action in the film, and love watching lots of Action films especially Akshay Kumar and now Tiger Shroff is huge by his MMA effects, and huge Fan of **DHOOM** mode.

On Dance experience with Hrithik Roshan , Vaani Kapoor replied on nervous mode "I wish that Could dance as perfect like him , But only best was that GROOVY step we did. On this Hrithik told , "Just Chill Have fun".

Then thought on shoot that I am literally having fun while dance but he is not, Hrithik is actually right. "

Also speaking on her Travels , Vaani tells only film Shamshera is shot entirely in Mumbai only. And **Priyanka Raina** tells Instinct that **Shamshera is first film to be shot in Ladakh.** On this Vaani replies but a very tiny part and I told to shoot full film there.

Having work with All the Leading Super heroes unlike Hrithik Roshan , Tiger Shroff , Ranbir Kapoor, Vaani tells that its very tough to define who is best . They are so perfect by their own means . Like Ranbir is sweet , Hrithik is just the best that anyone could dream and Did not have much scenes with Tiger Shroff, But I use to jot down on sets and He is very soft spoken and polite who is just dedicated to his work.

Director who is known for making films based on Travels and which also has a story that revolves around wonderful scenic locations, **Siddharth Anand** opens up that I treat my Locations as a Character in the film. I try and give my audience experience while sitting in the theater that they see the world. And if they see some locations that they haven't seen it before, Then indefinitely they ask me that **where Did you shoot that scene or song?** Then they decide to go there. This is something which I want to carry forward, Not many Directors in India are able to capture or showcase locations like which are a Treat to the eyes. **Showcase your locations well, Treat it as one of your characters,** "Give it importance s that is why People question me that I make films on Travels, That is my intent to showcase the world" Siddharth says with Exclamation.

Inspiration on Dialogues comes from Inder Raj Anand as He had written around 125 films which had powerful dialogues and If I write my dialogues in my film , so take inspiration from my Grand Father 's film only. Some of my films I like is Mard, Ek duje ke liye, KAALIA , SAFAR, Sangam and one was very small film **YEHI HAI ZINDAGI** which was a very small film , but it leaves a impact. It shows how to save money and what a family goes through.

Now Talking on **WAR**, War actually was a concept that came to me when I had lots of time after Bang Bang. That's time when I use to travel ,read lots of Books, My mind opened up with the exposure that Book gives you – Which I have never ever done in my life. I was never a reader, but I traveled, picked up books from Airport and I got excited by the Joyner of Spy Thrillers. Hence my idea of Heroes and stars changed by those books because films are One- Dimensional which encouraged me to come up with the story which was different.

Then another thing which comes into the mind is Actors, If Actors are 10 then Filmmakers are 100 and stars are just in numbers which can be counted on fingers. Although then too I wrote a story forgetting if I will get them or not, Keeping **Hrithik Roshan** in mind as had always a good association with Hrithik . I needed these two Actors which are Two Different CHARACTERS and If **Hrithik** is on One Hand , Then **Tiger Shroff** only has to be on Other Hand. As this is all about the pairing and we wont ever get a Better pair considering **HRITHIK vs TIGER** (Which also became one Catch line)

As story was about Mentor and Protege where He respects his Mentor , Gets inspire by his Mentor. In real life too Tiger is some what, so didn't want much to explain to audience about it. Audience has accepted that **Hrithik is IDOL for Tiger** and **HRITHIK vs TIGER** – Two Actors who are dedicated towards their work, Two Actors who can do any sorts of Action – makes easier for a filmmaker to concentrate on his subject then. **"Making film is of coarse tougher , But Handling Two actors is even more tougher. Its like handling Two wives at the end"**

CHAPTER TWENTY-FIVE

Discovering FICCI FRAMES and launch of Opera House

FiCCI FRAMES organized in a five star property at Powai included Filmmakers from all over nationally and internationally , where you can discuss lots more on Business of Cinema.

Also FICCI FRAMES established a special Bond with Rajshri Productions as was completely sitting with them and talking about Cinema through out the Three Day Festival

RajKumar Barjatya

Raj Kumar Barjatya , have been blessed to hear stories of "Vivah" through sir , The entire making process when sir was narrating scene by scene.gr
Also was blessed enough to be a part of Grand evnt when the Grand Opera House was launched with entire Indian Cinema

Priyanka Raina with Aamir Khan , Ashitosh Gowarikar, Ramesh Taurani, and many more at Opera House

With Bachchans at Opera House launch

Ambanis , Aamir Kan and Priyanka Raina at Grand Opera house launch

Bond with Deols

Here's a different bonding as guess was in eight standard and Sunny Deol had come to our school to shoot for his debut movie Dillagi. That was the time saw entire song shoot for full two weeks and couple of scenes too which were shot in school area.

Shooting song sequence with Bobby deol 'Koi nahi jo mujhe roke' for almost a week , I thought that 'filmmaking is not easy , song which we see in five minutes. This is the real hard work behind it'

And then interviewing Sunny Deol and Bobby Deol was almost a dream , whom saw the first ever live shoot

Sunny Deol, Priyanka Raina